Capacity for delight

Rachel Lark

Dear Dana —
Congratulations —
you are a fabulous
Stage Mom & actress
both. Eventually, I hope this
"First Edition", Typos
and all will be of
great value. In
the mean time
I hope it brings
you a laugh
or two.
Fondly,
#melissa

Please note, Match.com is a registered trademark.

Capacity for delight

Contact: Rachel.Lark@gmail.com

Author's note:

What you are about to read is my individual story. It should not be taken as a representation of anyone's experience except my own.

The opinions expressed here are my personal views and may not reflect those of anyone associated (or not associated) with Match.com.

The events I describe have not been exaggerated or invented for dramatic effect. This is the true story of the past two months of my life. The only fictional aspects are the names and minute details that I changed to protect the identities of the incredible men I met along the way.

I have no wish to expose or humiliate but rather, to share and illuminate.

I sincerely hope that the men, even those I only spent an hour or so with, got something out of our meeting as well.

Cheers,

Rachel

"Instructions for living a life:

Pay attention. Be astonished. Tell about it."

Mary Oliver

ONLINE DATING IS FOR LOSERS AND INTERNET PREDATORS

When I grow up, I want to be Stella Leoni.

Why?

Because she is an East Coast transplant thriving in Los Angeles as a young licensed architect.

It has been about six months since I earned my architectural degree and began logging the hours of work necessary to earn my professional license. Therefore, I need to stop saying, "when I grow up" because:

I have already "grown up"

or

I haven't "grown up" but should have.

Furthermore, the "when I grow up" statement just confuses me because, really, I want to be Stella Leoni (read between the lines: licensed architect) RIGHT NOW.

Patience is a virtue. I don't have it.

Stella, my personal mentor and professional supervisor at the Los Angeles architecture office where I consult (a fancy word for "work part time"), invited me to attend a networking event with her at a swanky Beverly Hills bar. Say hello to 600 young professionals, 400 of them men- in suits. Say hello to my fantasy.

As an awkward preteen, I used to look through Brooks Brothers catalogs for potential (hypothetical) husbands. I know, weird. I'd imagine the gentleman (never guy/dude) on page 8 to be a young lawyer, who enjoys afternoons on his sailboat, whisks me away to romantic cities, and, of course, serves me breakfast in bed.

Upon arriving at the party, Stella and I took a lap, our jaws dropped and obnoxious grins adorning our disbelieving faces. I know our jaws WERE dropped and our grins WERE obnoxious because we were approached by the host of the party. He kindly remarked that we should close our mouths and not make it SO obvious how much fun we were having.

Other people can see us? The fantasy catalog men know I'm gaping in awe?

Oops.

* * *

Later that night, back at Stella's apartment, we chatted while she got ready to see her boyfriend, who she met on Match.com. Studies show that 1 in 8 people will now meet their spouse on an online site. I have no idea if that's a fact, but it's what Stella told me, verbatim. Stella is social AND successful. Therefore Stella must know e v e r y t h i n g.

WAIT. Stop. REWIND.

"Her boyfriend who she met on Match.com."

BUT BUT BUT: I thought Match.com was for Internet predators, antisocial society rejects, and old men preying on young women.

Real people use online dating sites?

Someone I idolize found her charming, creative, cute boyfriend on such a site?

Deep breath. The world is still round, the sun still rises, and I still want to be Stella Leoni (though perhaps without the little "imperfect" detail about how she met her "perfect" boyfriend).

"We met online," sounds l a m e.

"We met at a professional networking event and I introduced myself because he looked like the page 8 Brooks Brothers catalog model I drooled over in middle school" sounds better.

"He cut in line in front of me at the grocery store", "he farted loudly at a funeral service and I laughed hysterically", "he thought I was hitting on him but really I just wanted to let him know he had toilet paper stuck to his shoe"–anything sounds better.

Sunday, January 17

CURIOSITY KILLED THE CAT

After a long, early morning run, I sit down at my laptop to check email. On a whim, out of morbid curiosity, I check out Match.com to see what this social reject network is all about.

Two hours later the sweat has dried on my face, my unstretched muscles are starting to freeze up, and I'm hooked. Totally sucked in.

Match.com is like attending a networking event, walking around with jaw dropped, and closely inspecting any attendee that catches my fancy.

(All without him or anyone else seeing me.)

Monday, January 18

SUBSCRIBED,
AND OUT TO SEA FOR MYSELF

I browse through my Facebook photos in an attempt to find some for my Match.com profile.

Note to self: NO CLEAVAGE.

(I'm still wary of perverts/Internet predators.)

I fool around with the search tool and manipulate it to suppose I'm a "male seeking female ages 24-25" to see what comes up. I want to check out my competition. Then I do another, more refined search, adding my interests and education level to the criteria. I want to see who comes up if a man searches for someone like me.

I conduct "stealth searches," feeling utterly sneaky, and find a few women I have a lot in common with and even some I think I could be friends with "in real life"... although most of them are showing a bit of cleavage in at least one of their photos. If they were my friends in real life, I would advise them that what they may deem "living on the edge," may in fact be "asking for attention from stalkers..."

Still, I decide to join my hopefully not "psycho sisters" online.

Step 1: I compose my profile.

Let's see, I'm "seeking" (Match.com uses this silly word; which seems to imply the use of binoculars) "a man aged 24-

30". Ideally 26-28, but the field only accepts numeric values, and there's no drop down bar to input "ideally".

This is what I come up with:

I'm easily inspired and easily enthused. I find beauty and excitement in every day. I smile, a lot. Common/compatible hobbies are nice but not necessary. However, I am looking for someone intelligent, with strong interests and passions. I rarely pass up an opportunity to learn something new, and see every experience as a potential source for inspiration and growth. I live a very busy/active lifestyle (running/traveling/exploring).

I love to study/practice design (I consult for an LA architect and just started a design collaborative- we are currently working on the interior design for a sustainable/green "showcase house") and am extremely driven. I tend to be attracted to those who are equally dedicated to their careers/professions.

Those who know me best (sorority sisters from college, family members, and close friends) have all told me that I am an extrovert. However, I have always considered myself an introvert. I enjoy quiet weekends reading (favorites: Henry James, Ayn Rand, Mary Oliver) in old libraries or at streetside café tables–but also love to host parties and get dolled up for "a night out on the town." Deep down inside, I believe I am a dork through and through. Don't be fooled, I think attending lectures, watching documentaries, and picnics in the park are all "fun" activities. I'm comfortable with who I am. I'm young and energetic, but my interests often align with those slightly beyond my years.

I'm new to LA, not sure what I'm looking for exactly, but would love to have someone to explore with and stir up some fun.

I hit "Submit."

My profile is PUBLIC!

I am the NEWEST she-fish in the e-sea!

ATTACK OF THE 33-YEAR-OLD MEN

Apparently, "seeking men 24-30" implies that 31-45-year-olds have a chance. WHAT?!

Profile refinement: I change "seeking men 24-30" to "seeking men 24-29," to deter the mid/late 30-year-olds and weirdo grandpapas.

I check my Match.com inbox (Match.com inbox = Match-box? Ooo I like that!).

Current messages = sixteen total, mostly from men over my posted age limit. Delete, delete, delete (repeat fifteen times).

I do, however, have the courtesy to hit "Politely Decline" and check the Age box in response to the creepy old dudes, so they know they were rejected due solely to a number (rather than something more personal, like their excessive chest hair or lazy eye).

ONE Message stands out:

Subject: WELCOME TO LA!

I am writing to you because you seem smart, interesting, and fun! Well, that AND the fact that you're beautiful, might as well be honest, right? Also, on your profile you mentioned your firm is designing a "showcase house" and I thought I'd give you the heads up that the AIA is currently accepting submissions for their spring home tour!

Oliver

Wow. This guy is giving me a gift "of my kind," a link, a potentially valuable piece of information, without any guarantee that I will even write back to him, let alone give him anything in return. Incredible.

With anticipation, I click to view his profile. My heart sinks. He's 30, and what's worse, he looks it. I'll have to mull this over.

I mentally add the adjective "older" to his name, because if I'm going to be corresponding with lots of men I've never met, I might as well tack descriptive adjectives to their names to help me to recall who is who.

I carry out a few targeted searches and go ahead and "favorite" a few of the guys (so that I can keep them on the "favorites list" for future consideration and possible daydreaming/emailing).

One of these "Match-men" with serious potential is Peter ("Paper Perfect Peter") a blond, sparkly blue-eyed 26-year-old. Peter is a second-year grad student, double majoring in biochemistry and molecular biology, who lists "the campus library" and "Bergamont Station Art Galleries" as his favorite places.

Sigh. I'm already drooling.

Then I read the Mika lyrics he's posted on his profile page:

"I've dreamt alone, now the dreams won't do."

My salivating syndrome has now progressed to full on… well, I'm ready to make out with the computer screen.

Twelve hours later I'm enthralled to find his profile photographs popping into my head (like my own little music video) during my morning run.

I send him a message telling him so.

We talk online and it goes a bit like (or exactly like) this:

Peter: so what got you on the site?

Me: a friend of mine had a great Match.com experience AND I meet the same people (or same type of people over and over again)...what about you?

Peter: same here! And I'm guessing I'm not going to find a MOMENTOUS relationship at a happy hour downtown one night…

Me: so that's what you're looking for... MOMENTOUS?

Peter: in nine letters, yes!

Me: that is QUITE a lot of pressure! lol

Peter: but wait, listen to what I mean by "MOMENTOUS"

Me: ok let's hear it. Webster style.

Peter: ok then... Let's see… I'm still refining it BUT here's what I have so far: MOMENTOUS (adj.): lively, enthusiastic about life and art, warm… the type who fills her life with good experiences and good people. Root: MOMENT (as in one that leads to many) + US (as in between two connected people)

…

Where did all the good guys go?! I know! I know!

The Internet. (?!)

FINGERS CROSSED FOR
A GOOD DOSE OF "MOMENTOUS"

Twenty-four hours after our online conversation, Paper Perfect Peter and I meet at The Yard for a drink.

I show caution by sending my mother his photo attached to the following email:

Tonight at 6 pm I will be meeting a guy named Peter (photo attached—if he doesn't resemble this photograph I will run—pepper spray in hand), at The Yard, in Santa Monica. If you don't hear from me by the morning, please present the cops with this email along with the attached photograph. XORL

I arrive at the date dressed to impress. I had an interview with a downtown architecture firm earlier in the day and had to drive straight from the meeting to The Yard. I'm secretly glad to have a legitimate reason to wear charcoal slacks, fashion-forward heels, and a sharp and structured blazer to our date. I feel powerful in blazers. I want a guy who wants a powerful woman, who finds power in a woman sexy, not intimidating. During my junior year of high school, I interned for a senator on Capitol Hill and had a weekly excuse to wear cufflinks. I didn't have any of my own, so I borrowed my father's. On interning days, before leaving the house in the morning, when it was still cold and early, I would quietly sneak into my parents' bedroom to pick out a pair of cufflinks from the box in my father's sock drawer. On my way out, I always sprayed my neck and wrists with my mother's perfume.

I always felt lovely doused in my mother's perfume (magic potion!) and powerful wearing my father's cufflinks (decorative armor!). I felt I could conquer the world. I wonder if Peter ever got a kick out of wearing his father's cufflinks, though I hope he didn't wear his mother's perfume.

I find Peter waiting just outside the gastro-pub's door. I recognize his blond locks and bright blue eyes from his photographs immediately. I extend my hand and introduce myself; it seems proper that I'm dressed for an interview. Isn't that what a first date is, anyway?

We sit at the bar and each order a glass of wine. The Yard is one of those restaurants that's small enough for every table to be within easy earshot of every other table but intimate enough in "atmosphere" for every couple at every table to feel that their conversations are private.

"When did you move to LA and what brought you to The Valley?" Pete asks.

"I graduated from architecture school in May and moved to California in June. I live with my aunt and uncle, and intend to remain with them until I score the "full-time long-term job" and then decide what part of town I should move to. In the meantime, it's been really nice to be with family for my first few seasons out of school and on a new coast. It also doesn't hurt that my uncle keeps a bar stocked with the finest wines and that there's a pool and grill ideal for hosting parties in the backyard. I realize I'm very lucky in regards to my situation. You live here in Santa Monica, right?" I ask.

"Yes, I live here because I love the beach and I love to surf. When I'm not in class, I'm usually surfing or playing tennis. I turned down a full-ride collegiate tennis scholarship because I wanted to pursue my academic interests. So now I study mostly and play tennis when I have time, rather than the reverse."

"I work mostly, and have fun with friends when I have time, but sometimes I wish that was the reverse," I say.

He chuckles and asks, "So, tell me how your interview went."

I reply, "The closest public parking was half a mile away, so I had to trek quite an uncomfortable distance, considering I was wearing heels and it was pouring rain. I arrived drenched and had to dry my blazer in the women's restroom by crouching under the hand air blower."

"Oh wow, I'm really sorry," he says.

"Oh no! I wasn't complaining! I found the whole thing a bit comic, really. And the interview itself went very well, and that's really all that matters!" I reply.

I tend to leave excellent impressions on interviewers. I hope that means that I'm a rockstar at first dates, too.

"I think it's really awesome that you're in the field of architecture. I've always been fascinated by science, but also harbor a strong interest in fine art. I know those usually don't go hand in hand, but for me they always have," he says.

Wow. I've never been on a date with someone who was so perfect on paper. And, since I knew about his background and interests before meeting him, he is in many ways "prescreened" to pass my "first round of tests".

Also, he's read my profile and is therefore privy to a "cheat sheet" outlining exactly what I'm looking for. Perhaps this means he's fast-tracked to get an "A" in my course.

At the end of the date, he escorts me to my car. As we say goodbye, he puts on his glasses so he can drive home. His glasses are really geeky, and I think he looks cuter with them on. I think he's aware that I'm thinking about how cute his geeky glasses are. He blushes. I tell him that I had a nice time and would like to see him again. He says the sentiment is mutual.

In the seclusion of my car, I wonder if he and I have any chemistry. That's not something I could predict from paper. I want to walk back into the bar to ask the bartender (who was shamelessly watching our date unfold) if she thought she saw a spark or if we just seemed like two like-minded magnets trying to connect but configured to repel.

I drive to my grandparents' apartment to crash for the night because I've had a marathon of a day and they live close to where I have to work tomorrow morning.

Before going to bed, I check my Match-box, with Grandma Rose inquisitively looking over my shoulder. I explain the "30-year-old Older Oliver" predicament to her.

I show her his profile. I read her the email he sent me containing the architecture submission link.

She adores him.

Sitting Indian-style in pink striped pajama shorts and one of my many well-worn sorority spring break T-shirts, I stare at Older Oliver's photo on my grandmother's dated PC computer screen and ask, "But is he too old for me?"

"You know what, Rachel," she says,

"I think he looks and seems a bit like your uncle Jake."

These words are magic to my ears. I wonder if she knew the effect those exact words would have on me.

Uncle Jake is charming, patient, giving, and bright. I know that I want to someday marry a man just like my uncle Jake. Uh-oh…

Under the spell of her commentary, I go back and read Oliver's profile again. I note:

I'm attracted to women who are witty, fun, and confident. I'm looking for a woman who feels just as gorgeous in a T-shirt and shorts as she does all done up for a night out. If you can beat me at cards/trivia/anything I'll think it's sexy—not intimidating.

I love how he says he wants someone who feels "gorgeous in a T-shirt and shorts" rather than someone who is "gorgeous in a T-shirt and shorts."

He sounds like he's looking for the right things in a woman. So I write back:

For the category of best message, you win. Don't you hate it when people send you Match.com messages in which it's apparent they didn't really read your profile? Or, even more bizarre, when they talk only about themselves with no reference to you or potential common interests? THANK YOU for the lead! I am aware of those AIA tours, but unfortunately they are for new construction/architecture, whereas this house was a renovation/interior design/retrofit project. But really—very kind of you and I am sincerely appreciative.

In conclusion, I will mention that you are the only 30-year-old I have responded to. I'm just going to throw that out there.

Cheers,

Rachel

TIME MOVES MORE QUICKLY ON THE INTERNET

Twelve hours later I'm arranging to meet Older Oliver face to face.

In the meantime, I give my mother a list of "user names" of men that have contacted me and ask her to check them out and let me know who to investigate for further consideration. The number of messages piling up in my Match-box is overwhelming. She is more than willing to help me sort through them all and separate the valuable content from the junk mail.

Further, this escapade is turning out to be an opportunity for her to indulge and play Matchmaker and attempt to set me up with who she wants me to be with (sans the awkward blind dates). I tell her I'm open to her suggestions; I feel no angst because I can screen their profiles before agreeing to contact the men she suggests!

She has a field day and emails me a list of usernames to search. Upon close examination of their profiles, I find a motorcycle in one of the photographs. From an early age, my parents hammered it into my head that "MOTORCYLES ARE DANGEROUS AND WILL KILL YOU, FURTHERMORE BOYS WHO PLAY WITH THEM ARE MORONS."

I call her out on it.

Her response: "Oh, but he looks hottttt!!!"

Ok then…

I recommence sorting through messages.

Apparently, Match.com is a little snitch: it notifies those users you add to your Favorites list. Dammit.

Or not. A message has arrived from Lucas, a 28-year-old actor (yuck) who I favorited because, well, just read what his profile says:

Me: laid back, easy to get along with, quick to laugh, driven, loving, audiophile, intelligent, hard-working, trustworthy, fit, creative, musical, and I will make you laugh. I usually hear that I bring out the weird in people and that I come across much older than I am. My parents are still together after thirty-five years and my brother has always been and always will be one of my best friends in the world. I'm kind of obsessed with the Argentine Tango. Also, don't mistake my lack of drinking/drugs/smoking as being boring. I don't drink coffee because I have enough energy as it is. I don't drink alcohol because I'm retarded enough as it is. I've never done drugs because I like my brain the way it is. I'm basically the nice guy who'll challenge you and laugh with you. You: independent, intelligent, funny, trustworthy, trusting, fit, cheerful.

His message to me:

What are you doing in West Hills? Match told me you favorited me, so I read your profile and thought, "Holy crap. She actually seems great."

Suddenly, I'm superstoked that Match.com is a BIG snitch.

Tra-la-la-BOOM-de-ay!

I immediately write back to "Laughing Lucas."

MY FIRST EXPERIENCE WITH AN "OLDER MAN"

I meet Older Oliver at a coffee shop in Westwood. When I arrive, he is already there, waiting on the lower level. From the raised entry landing, I can see out over the tables, over the heads of the other patrons, and awkwardly let my eyes settle on Oliver's (receding) hairline. I take a deep breath, thinking this is a BIG mistake.

I walk over to his table and introduce myself. Oliver has dark eyes, darker lashes, and thick eyebrows. He looks a bit like Nicholas Cage. Why reference a movie star to convey his look? Well, to be quite frank, because I don't watch much TV/many movies. So, I am fairly confident that everyone who reads this, even those who've spend the past seven months on a remote desert island, will be able to recognize any star I refer to.

Ironically, many of my friends now work in the entertainment industry (probably because most of the population of Los Angeles works in the entertainment industry). They find my complete obliviousness to celebrity completely baffling. They even have a joke: how do you tell an A-list celebrity from a B-list one? See if Rachel Lark can recognize them.

Thanks to my best LA friend, Tess, I stood on the red carpet just feet away from Tom Hanks. Apparently, there were also about fourteen other celebrities equidistant, but I was completely ignorant of their identities. For Christmas, our friend Nicole sent out a card with a photo of her and one of this year's most recognizable TV stars on the front. The back read: "Happy Holidays from the two of us." On receiving it, I immediately called Tess to get the scoop on "Nicole's cute new boyfriend." My inquiry was met with wild laughter. I didn't get it. I had to assure her that, no; I don't live in a TV-less igloo. I just choose not to watch it.

Mr. Cage/Older Oliver and I proceed to the coffee counter. We order our coffee, find a table, and begin talking. Oliver's voice is OCTAVES lower than Perfect Pete's. It's deep and incredibly masculine. I like it.

Because Older Oliver seems very clever (or perhaps I assume extra years equal extra wisdom), I ask him if he knows why an overwhelming number of 35-year-old men have messaged me even though my profile clearly states "seeking men ages 24-29."

He replies, "Because they assume those parameters aren't set in stone. Especially since there are women on Match.com who are seeking men 'between 6'2 and 6'6,' which makes sense if the woman herself is tall, but many of these women are only 5'2". Sometimes the 'rules' don't make sense. Why shouldn't a 5'8" guy contact a 5'2" girl?"

He makes a great point. I tell him so and then ask, "And what about the messages from men that contain no personal information. Messages all about themselves, with no reference to me, or what we might have in common. I actually suspect these men must just copy and paste these vague and overly generic messages to many women. What about that?"

Older Oliver shakes his head a bit, smiles, and explains, "Because of society's convention of men pursuing women, most women aren't proactive, even on Match.com, about making that first point of contact. While you may experience an overwhelming response and number of messages from interested men, men receive far fewer unsolicited messages. If a man sends five emails, he's lucky if one woman responds. So why should they invest a lot of time crafting intricate, personal messages only to be blatantly ignored? Better to send something quick, and IF she takes the bait, proving mutual interest, then it makes sense for him to really invest the time and effort to "woo her with words," so to speak."

I'm intrigued to be getting the inside scoop on Internet dating from the OTHER (male) perspective. And I'm intrigued that I find Older attractive. No, really. Just by virtue of his age, I can't believe I'm truly attracted to him. And he's not "hot" like all of the "boys" I've dated thus far.

He's different. He's manlier. "Hot" would not even apply; in fact he's NOT hot. He's… handsome.

I feel good with him. Comfortable. At ease. Happy.

The way he sticks up for the other men on Match is charming. His answers and rationales are clever. The way he carefully considers my questions and smiles when he answers is very endearing.

My grandmother was right.

At the end of the night I'm not sure if he's right for me, but I do know I want to see him again.

And I'm still digesting the fact that he's 30… and that I'm attracted to him.

From my car, I call my mom to tell her that I've just had coffee with a GREAT guy. That he's SO GREAT that I wish I'd meet him five years from now when I myself will be more mature. When I am ready for "A GREAT GUY," not just seeking something fun/hot/exciting/youthful…

I ask her, "Should I be totally transparent with Older Oliver and tell him that I had a great time but that I'm still mulling it over?"

Without hesitating she replies, "NO. Men don't want to hear about that. They have to put up with it enough once they're married. You don't need to overanalyze this and come to immediate conclusions and share those conclusions with him. Besides, what's so wrong with just truthfully telling him you had a great time and would enjoy seeing him again? And letting him feel GOOD rather than following it by 'but I'm not sure if you're THE ONE'… and bursting his bubble? Think about it, Rachel."

"Point taken. Thanks, Mom," I reply.

She continues, "Also, your own brother has a receding hairline, and he's 21. SO, you need to get a grip, missy."

Again, she's right.

I reply, "Second point taken. Thanks again, Mom."

I turn onto Wilshire, toward Tess's apartment. Tess moon-walked into my life over a decade ago. I say "moonwalk" partly because he loves Michael Jackson, but mostly because she doesn't really "walk" in the conventional and purely functional sense. Rather, she abruptly transitions from one pose/strut to the next. This proves to be quite "attention catching," and it's further exacerbated by the (in most cases inappropriately loud) volume of her voice.

Her family moved from Pennsylvania to my hometown in northern Virginia just before the start of sixth grade. I've always had a soft spot for the perceived underdog, and therefore I consistently sought out the "new kids." At the age of 12, I took her under my wing, and we became best friends.

At the end of the year, graduating from elementary school, we promised each other we'd stay best friends and remain close. As it happened, our attempts to make new friends proved to be enough of a distraction for us to completely lose touch after the first day of middle school.

It was not until I moved to Los Angeles and mentioned my move on Facebook that Tess (who had moved to Los Angeles herself the previous year) took the initiative and made contact.

I found myself in a new city reunited with an old best friend. I believe the chemistry you have with your best friends does not expire or diminish with time. When Tess and I met, we had friendship chemistry, and now that we are both in our early twenties, I find her often offensive and inappropriate comments to be just as humorous and amusing as I did back in elementary school. We have just as much fun together as we did before (although now our fun has the potential to get us into a lot more trouble).

Tess and I got a second chance at one of our first friendships. This time around, it's Tess's turn. Ever since I landed in Los Angeles, she has taken ME under HER wing.

Once I arrive at her adorable Westside apartment, I tell her all about my Match.com experience thus far.

Her reaction: much squealing at her standard (ear-shattering) volume. She wants to see PHOTOS. I log into Match.com and navigate to Perfect Peter's page. Her reaction: MORE squealing at a volume never before heard by human ears.

I tell her that there are more men on this site just as cute as Peter. There are so many, in fact, I've had to enlist my own mother to help me sift through them. There are about a BAZILLION times more SUPERFISH in the sea than we thought.

She goes GAGA.

She can't believe I've been on the site less than a week and have had two dates, one of which was with a 30-year-old. She wants to know if she can pick from the "leftover" men that I don't want to go on second dates with. She wants to know if I'll screen, interview, and then hand off guys to her. Apparently I could be the guinea pig for the ladies of LA's Westside…

We sip wine and browse the profiles of the men who've "winked" at me on Match. "Winking" is like "poking" on

Facebook. It's just another method of contact, though perhaps a slightly more suggestive one...

The combination of holding wineglasses and shopping for bachelors proves to be dangerously messy. Each time I click past a Match profile without looking at the photos, Tess raises her arms, spills her wine, and shouts, "GO BACK!"

We read Laughing Lucas's reply to my latest message (in which I suggest we meet). He proposes we meet at a "Star Party," explaining:

It's this really cool deal at the Observatory where a bunch of people from the LA Astronomical Society (typically anywhere from 20-50) bring their telescopes and set them out on the lawn from mid-afternoon until nighttime for anybody to come look through. Happens once a month.

http://www.griffithobservatory.org/pstarparties.html

- Closet Astronomy Nerd

Tess and I react in unison: "Awwwwww"!

Tuesday, January 23

I'D RATHER CONVERSE WITH CURATORS THAN GORILLAS

Apparently, when men list their height as 5'8" in their profiles, they really mean 5'7½".

And so when women include "outdoors" in their profiles, men assume that means they want to climb Mount Everest. Daily.

I know this is the case because I've received quite a few invitations for "extreme outdoor adventure" first dates. So, after my morning run, I sit down and refine my profile by adding the following:

NEW ADDITIONAL NOTE: In response to the "Tarzans" mistaking me for their ideal "Jane," I feel obliged to clarify: By outdoors I mean I love orchards/vineyards/the feel of the sun on my skin/the incredible sensation of an outbreak of rain completely drenching me in the middle of a long run/spending afternoons reading & writing in a park/exploring urban streets on foot/attending outdoor music or cultural festivals. I do NOT mean sky diving/week-long whitewater rafting trips/camping. Sorry, I don't want to give the wrong impression! Okay? wink wink nod nod...BIG smile!

That afternoon I meet Laughing Lucas at the planetarium. He's very fair-skinned, with blue eyes and a little bit of blond scruff (but well kept, nothing close to a full-on mustache/gruff cave-man beard). Yes, he's four years older than I, but his face radiates with childlike whimsy and inquisitiveness. He's thin but not gaunt; rather it seems that "light" is the right word. As if he's the ideal build for effortless dancing, even in the streets like Freddy in the musical My Fair Lady.

He is cinematic, loud, funny, and vibrant. He's a natural comic, animated in his gestures, and acrobatic with his facial expressions. My relatives have openly "poo-pooed" the idea of my dating an actor, so I put up my best attempt to NOT like him but find myself giving in. He exceeds the claim he makes in his Match profile. Not only does he make me laugh, but I laugh more than I've laughed in the previous six weeks — in total.

I ask him how long he's been on Match (since September) and how many people he's met in person (two). He turns the questions around and asks me.

With reddening ears I say, "I've been on Match for about five days, and this... well, this is my third date." I don't mention that I fully intend to meet Paper Perfect Peter later, bringing my total to four dates in five days. I continue, "You could say that I'm having a lot of fun with it." I muster my most winning, BIGGEST smile. We both break into laughter.

Full chest, deep belly laughter.

"But really," I go on to explain, "this week has been incredible. I've never met so many intelligent, witty, NICE guys in such a short amount of time. I'm meeting great people who I wouldn't have the opportunity to meet in a different context, whether it be because they're too busy, work too much, or our paths just wouldn't cross. I'm meeting people outside my current social circles. It's exciting and refreshing."

He replies, "Yeah, the social circle thing is a bit of an issue. I meet a lot of really awesome people daily, but ninety-nine percent of them are people I work with. It's not really that great an idea to date them."

"Agreed!" I look around the dimly lit room filled with spotlighted plants. "Do you think that there are certain Match.com date hotspots?"

"What do you mean?" He exaggeratedly furrows his brow.

"Well, there have to be a few obvious choices for places to meet. So, it could be probable during a Match.com date to see other Match.com members that I recognize from their profile pictures. They too could be at that very venue, having their own Match.com first date! Wouldn't that be bizarre?"

"What would you do in that situation?" he asks.

"I'd introduce myself so the four of us could all meet. It's more efficient. Only makes sense."

Again, we're both laughing very hard, and our faces are very red.

When we finish viewing the exhibits, we walk to his car so he can drive me to mine. He starts the car and a strange voice booms from the speakers.

"Sorry, audiobook," he says, blushing.

I LOVE audiobooks. TEN points for him. Seriously.

He pulls up to my car, and as I step out, I find myself babbling with emphasis and without reservation, "I had SO MUCH FUN and I'd LOVE to meet you here again!" Perhaps his dramatics are contagious. I get into my car feeling pleasantly charmed by both my first visit to the planetarium and by my first date with Laughing Lucas.

I sit still, smiling for a moment, then dial Paper Perfect Peter. He'd had obligations at the Bio-lab this morning, so we discussed meeting in the early evening. He suggests LACMA (the Los Angeles County Museum of Art, my favorite place in LA). Apparently the only place to find really nice guys IS the Internet!

En route, I call Stella (my trusted adviser AND the one who got me into this multimen-Match-mess in the first place) to ask how many dates I can go on with Perfect Peter/ Laughing Lucas/Older Oliver before I have to:

A. decide which one I'm really "serious" about

B. tell them that I'm going on dates with lots of men

C. narrow it down to just one.

According to Stella, it's not "serious" until I'm speaking with these men daily. By her definition, at this point I'm not at risk of "leading them on." First dates don't need to end in finite conclusions and long-term predictions. Besides, for all I know, they are hanging out with other women and mixed up in Match-mayhem as well. Stella (reminder: Stella knows EVERYTHING) reassures me that I am overanalyzing and shouldn't be worrying about this and should just have FUN with it.

ROCK ON.

I meet Perfect Peter at the LACMA and we have a subperfect time. He shares stories from his past with me (most of which he finds hilarious) while we stroll between exhibits. All of his stories bore me to the point of agitation. I'm bummed. I want to like him! The fact that I had a merely OKAY time at my FAVORITE LA venue proves that he and I are NOT meant to be.

He's good-looking. And smart. And fit. And kind.

But it's apparent we don't have chemistry. At all.

Whether or not I'm attracted to someone has very little to do with how conventionally attractive they are. Rather, it's directly correlated to how I perceive their attractiveness. The teenage-mutant-ninja-turtle-like men that some of my friends find HOT HOT HOT I find GROSS GROSS GROSS. I seem to be attracted to the men that my friends view as "dorky." But I'm not looking for someone that everyone is attracted to. I'm just looking for that special attraction that's both for, and in, my eyes only.

On our way out of the LACMA and into the parking lot, we bump into a few of Peter's friends. He introduces me, and they invite us to stay for the film showing that night. I decline and mention I'm tired. Peter has an early morning (more lab hours), so he also declines and walks me to my car. We have one of those sterile "good-byes," where both parties know there won't be much future contact, if any.

I get home and sink into my bed. A text arrives from an unknown number:

"Hey LACMA gal. I'm hanging out with a bunch of friends and Peter said you're fun. Come meet up."

I'm a bit freaked out.

Either:

A. "No-Longer-Perfect Peter" gave one of his friends my number without asking my permission

Or

B. One of his friends stole it

Both scenarios make me very uncomfortable. Since I've decided Peter isn't my type, I'm considering asking him if I may give Tess his number. Who knows, maybe she'll respond better to his "humor." But note, I fully intend to ask him before giving his number out. It's just common courtesy.

I respond to the unknown texter:

"Who is this? Sorry I'm in for the night!"

The mystery man writes back immediately:

"Stay warm lil mama, we'll hang out another time."

FOUL. I'm officially 110% sketched out. I ask:

How did you get my number?

Again, immediate response:

"I don't easily take no for an answer."

Okay, I'm totally freaked out. I text Peter, asking if he gave out my number. He doesn't reply.

As I reach to drop my phone on the nightstand, a text arrives from Laughing Lucas:

"I really enjoyed meeting you and look forward to seeing you again."

I turn off my phone and put it on the table. I lay down and close my eyes. Big smile. Sweet dreams.

THIS ADVENTURE
NOW REQUIRES A BINDER

Today I have plans to meet Tess for a day at the spa. I make myself late printing out the profiles of the guys I've met thus far (Laughing Lucas, Perfect Peter, Older Oliver) AND the ones I've made plans to meet this coming week (Motivated Mark and Woodlands Will).

I take the printed sheets and put them in a mini binder for two reasons:

1. I'm starting to worry about keeping the different guys straight.

2. I want Tess's (always uncensored) opinion(s).

First up at the spa: JACUZZI. There are two Jacuzzis, one for talking and one for SILENCE. We would probably survive only about forty-five seconds in the silent Jacuzzi before being kicked out partly due to our age, as we haven't yet mastered volume control (although I doubt Tess ever will), and partly due to MATCH.COM. I have TOO much to tell her, and it's TOO exciting to whisper.

I begin to reveal the events of my first Match-week. After a few minutes, I notice I've attracted a small audience of naked ladies (of varying ages, apparent by the varying length of their in some cases sagging b...). I am fascinated by my sudden status as "orator of the naked old ladies." It seems my escapades have multigenerational appeal.

An hour later, flushed from the Jacuzzi and steam rooms, Tess and I venture to the outdoor sundeck's lounge chairs, where I share the profiles of the various men (with their photographs displayed).

Tess is drooling.

She asks, without a hint of sarcasm in her tone, "Now that you've decided Paper-Perfect Peter isn't your cup of tea, can I have him?"

I tease, "I'm not sure he's mine to give!"

She persists, "Rachel, SHARING is CARING."

"I'll consider it," I say.

She continues, "Fine, that's all I ask. Also, PLEASE tell me you are blogging about this somewhere."

I shake my head.

She sits upright on her lounge chair (tangling herself in the oversized spa robe in the process) and exclaims, "YOU NEED TO START WRITING ABOUT THIS. NOW. OR YESTERDAY. I'm telling you Rachel, GET ON IT."

I agree to start keeping a journal and explain, "Honestly, in the context of my life, usually only one decent guy is on my horizon at a time. So, traditionally at this point, I'd be asking myself if the (albeit temporary) addition of boyfriend X improves my quality of life. The answer would be YES, concerning most of the suitable 'boyfriend bachelors' I have met this week. However, thanks to Match.com, there's not just ONE on the horizon. I have options. I don't need to settle for the one decent option; rather, I get to CHOOSE among many. Or, not even CHOOSE but KEEP LOOKING. These guys are mostly good and potentially FANTASTIC, so I don't feel like I have to settle for less than a fantastic relationship. This is unprecedented."

Tess agrees. "Putting extreme effort into liking the one on the horizon is the NORM because usually there aren't multiple guys to pursue at once!"

"I know," I say. "God bless Match.com."

On my way home from the spa, I call to see if my grandparents are at my aunt and uncle's house yet. If so, I wonder if they are all discussing my Match-quest. My cousin Kate answers and exclaims: "Hey, Rachel! I hear you're an Internet slut!"

Great…

Apparently it has been THE topic of discussion and has been a bit exaggerated. You'd think I was sleeping with the Match-men instead of just having coffee.

I laugh lightly, thinking that if I were sleeping with all these men, I'd end up on one of those "who's my baby's [Internet?] daddy" episodes of Maury. THEN my relatives could justifiably call me an "Internet slut."

When I pull into the driveway, I send a message to the mystery texter from last night:

"I need to know who you are and how you got my number… not joking around."

He responds:

"Peter went home to bed because he had an early morning but we all went to party and he said I could see if you wanted to come. Call you later."

I attempt to add him into my phone contacts as "Match Stalker" so I can recognize his number in the future AND because he still hasn't told me his name, yet he's sent me multiple text messages. I've been adding the prefix "Match" to all the contacts I've added to my phone this week. Yes, the M section in my phone reads: "Match Peter," "Match Lucas," "Match Oliver"…

An hour later the mystery texter writes:

"WHAT?"

His message doesn't make sense, so I reread our string of texts. Apparently, rather than adding him to my phone book as "Match Stalker," I sent him the message:

"MATCH STALKER."

Crap.

Great, I've pissed off the sketchy-stalker. I don't want to risk egging him on, so I decide not to respond.

When I get home, I pull Match.com up on my laptop and speed through profiles so my aunt and grandmother can see what it's all about.

They think I don't spend enough time viewing the profiles of the men that have written to me. I explain that I don't have three hours a day to waste on Match.com. That doesn't resemble life. That more closely resembles an Internet addiction.

I continue to go through the new emails with them while they look over the young men. I check out the guys who have shown "interest" in me. One of them really strikes me. His profile reads:

My name is Alex. I'm a 25-year-old career-oriented college grad with lots of hobbies, lots of friends, and an enthusiasm for life and adventure. I was brought up in a small town with old-fashioned values and I've never forgotten a single thing my father taught me. I've since moved to the city which I now call home and which I will continue to explore until I'm no longer able. I live a high-energy, fast-paced life.

Here's a bit about the person I hope to find:

I'm looking for someone who can keep up, pushes herself to try new things, and challenges me. She is as passionate as I am about travel and learning and will take an intense interest in my life but be capable of charting her own course and pursuing her own hobbies/career as well. She is well spoken, strong willed, and won't back down from an argument but will be rational and able to admit when she's wrong. She works hard to realize her dreams but takes the time to enjoy life and all it has to offer.

Does this intimidate you? Then you're probably not who I'm looking for. On the other hand, if your blood started boiling because I just described you and you're angry that you can't prove it at this very instant, you should probably send me a message. We have a lot to talk about.

The most important thing for you to know about me is that I love my life far too much not to share it with someone. I'll talk to anyone, any time, so send me a message!

Before I know it, I'm emailing him:

Subject: Responses to your profile

I too am a [24]-year-old career-oriented college grad with lots of hobbies, lots of friends, and an enthusiasm for life.

I am incredibly high energy, and usually have 2 more things on my plate than I should (or 2 more than the "average" person would). I don't believe in settling for average in anything. Sometimes mediocrity drives me insane.

Although... my jogging pace is about a 9:45min/mile- and for some reason I'm quite content with that. Perhaps I am full of contradictions.

I've always been passionate about travel (lived in Switzerland for 6 months) and learning (attended an all-girls prep school and then went on to study architecture at Virginia Tech, at the time ranked #1 in the US for undergraduate architecture- GO HOKIES!).

I work hard and sometimes spend TOO much time on my work and have to be reminded to "take a break." I love what I do and have a hard time walking away from it. I'm looking for someone who is as passionate about his career/hobbies as I am about mine, but reminds me to "take a break," have some fun, and STOP and recognize that (although I'm always working toward "what comes next") where I am HERE and NOW is pretty spectacular.

Relationships often inspire me to pause—"put down my pencil"—and unwind. To get me outside of my own head/work. To enjoy the things in everyday life that are universally enjoyable.

I can hold my own in a disagreement, but if you yell/raise your voice I may start crying... or walk out the door (maybe even with running shoes in hand to go "run it out" and "cool off"). I'd like someone with opinions, but not someone who is "argumentative."

I too, love my life.

Your words intimidate me a little bit. Maybe. But intimidation or not, I'm impressed. So I'm writing.

My brow is furrowed... my aunt is here and just commented that I look peeved. So maybe I am angry? I don't get angry often. I smile, almost always. Sometimes my face gets sore from TOO much smiling.

Regardless of whether or not we have potential, you sound interesting.

At the very least we could meet for a cup of coffee and insightful conversation (tea for me, thanks).

Hope you enjoyed this novel. (lol)

cheers,

Rachel

At first I'm really excited about this one. But then the words from his profile start to sink in and land shakily in the pit of my stomach. I'm reminded of the way an ex-boyfriend of mine used to talk. Internet or no Internet, this is still a search for a real relationship, and I don't want to repeat my mistakes from relationships past. Wouldn't it be something if even though I'm using a new method of meeting guys, I still select the "winners" that will leave me "losing"?

I once read an article that explained that some women who've been in unhealthy relationships seek future unhealthy relationships. They do this because of a subconscious desire to recreate an experience that ended negatively in the hopes of a second chance in which it may end positively. Hence, some women aren't looking for a "good guy" but rather a "bad guy" that they can make "good."

I'm not saying the ex-boyfriend that broke my heart was a "bad" guy. I'm just saying that in the end, he was "bad"/wrong for me. I don't want to subconsciously choose a guy just like the one I first fell in love with in order to craft a different ending to the beginning of a story that I've already lived.

So half an hour later I'm at it again, and send Adventure Alex another message:

Subject: On second thought...

If you're looking for someone for you to challenge... then I'm not the girl for you.

Been there, dated that.

I challenge myself, I motivate myself, I push myself. That energy/those standards come from within. I'm not looking for someone else to do that. I'm looking for someone to encourage me, support me (emotionally), celebrate with me (my own achievements, their achievements, as well as just celebrate the wonders of everyday life), intrigue me (intellectually), and inspire me.

Ideally, I'd like someone who, after getting to know me, believes I'm more than capable of achieving everything I've set my mind to (especially, on the occasional instances when I'm either worn out to the point of second-guessing, or just having trouble being patient with the pace of life).

2 emails in less than an hour!? If I'm interested in something, I don't hold back. I pursue it.

Are YOU intimidated?

Cheers,

Rachel

WOODLAND CREATURES

I consult for an architect part-time. This means that some days I don't have to go to the office. Today is not one of those days.

Today work is s l o w . I venture to Match.com.

A new message from Adventure Alex greets me:

Subject: Breath of fresh air...

Hi Rachel! First of all, thank you so much for the email(s). You joked about writing a novel, but the attention you paid to your messages tells me that you're serious about this whole thing and really helps me paint a picture of who you are.

I wanted to tell you that my profile is written the way it is specifically to intimidate, to deter the average passer-by who is not willing to put the time and energy into finding out what I'm all about. I should tell you however that I'm probably not quite as intimidating as I come off in my profile.

The fact that you are driven, and hold yourself to high standards tells me that you're exactly the type of person I'm interested in getting to know. You say that you're not looking for someone to push you. I would point out that I'm not necessarily looking for someone to push. In fact, quite the opposite. I'm looking for someone who is self-motivated and has enough energy and motivation inside her that I will benefit just from being in her presence.

That said, I rather enjoy (and like to think that I'm quite good at) being supportive and uplifting. And for what it's worth, celebrating achievements is high on my list of past times... right under actually doing the achieving :). Trust me, nothing would make me happier than to be with someone I can be proud of and whose accomplishments I will undoubtedly tout to no end.

I'm sorry, this email is getting fairly long as well. I just want to make sure after your second email that I have at least attempted to address some of your concerns. Clearly I'm very interested in continuing this discussion and hopefully in meeting you in person. That brings me to the tricky part...

I hesitate to mention this especially after your remark about Tarzan and Jane but I'm actually in quite a remote part of Kenya at the moment. I will be here for the next week and am unreachable by phone, but thanks to this nifty satellite I obviously have Internet access. Please feel free to respond to this email and while I may not respond with the same expediency as I would stateside, I should have the opportunity to get back to you in less than 12 hours.

I hope this email finds you well,

Alex

Ok, so maybe he's NOT a mistake from relationships past? I'm squirming at my desk. And writing back- passionately!

Subject: RE: and you thought the 1st was long...

Glad you didn't mind the length. And now you know, I'm VERBOSE.

Usually, most people don't want to go out on a limb for fear of rejection. That's not an issue for me.

I WANT to put myself out there- so you can get an idea of who I am. If I'm not for you- then I wouldn't want to be with you... you know? Maybe you know something about YOU that would make us non-compatible. Or maybe we could get along GRANDLY... It takes 2 to make these calls. :)

Re: your intimidation profile factor: That is a great deterrence method- and really smart. I like it. I might have to add some "spikes" to mine. I continuously refine it- in order to shape the form of the replies...

I'm glad you are not intimidating in real life. I'm a very warm person although I can be distant when I'm working. However, I am incapable of being cold, unkind, or harsh...

I want someone who yes, takes pride in the accomplishments I strive to achieve- but who loves to be with ME at the end of the day... when I come home and I'm just "Rachel."... affectionate, energetic, in awe of life, curious, BIG SMILE... not defined by anything else... I want a guy who loves to be with JUST that.

And too, on the rare occasions that I'm the second guessing, questioning, pondering, exhausted, needing a HUG... THAT Rachel... I want someone who wants to cheer up/snuggle with/re-inspire/re-energize/encourage THAT Rachel too.

I'm not sure if I'm making sense... what I mean is that I push myself towards certain achievements and would want someone who could be proud of those achievements and encouraging... but not like me BECAUSE of them.

Or even someone who finds beauty/amusement/delight in my self perceived "flaws." No one is perfect, and I consider myself a work in progress. :)

I've got the "being a productive/efficient/motivated person" thing down pat. But taking the time to just "be a human being," I need to be reminded. Relationships assist by reminding me everyday, to stop and find beauty in the little things.

I like to be around people I'm proud of. I like to surround myself with people from whom I can learn something. Or many things. I'm hungry for knowledge. I will be a "life long learner," like my paternal grandparents (who are in their 70's and take history courses at Columbia University for fun).

What brings you to Kenya?

You said "nifty." Hahaha. That's a good word.

The only disappointment I found when reading your profile: you don't list museums and art as an interest. Oh well... the Getty Museum hosts evening live concerts in the summer months with a cocktail bar and all- so could that fall under the "Music and concerts" category I see listed under your interests? Wink wink?

There's more in your profile I want to discuss but I need to get back to work.

Let's have a cup of coffee when you return to the states?

safe travels,

Rachel

This guy... could be... as Perfect Peter put it: MOMENTOUS.

My romantic thoughts are interrupted by the arrival of a new Matchbox message. I click to open it.

Subject: hey...

Deep down inside... I think I am also a definite dork. However, on the surface I am also a dork.

Reading, watching documentaries, and lectures are fun? Well, I enjoy riding my shopping cart to my car like a five-year-old. But I think I've already mentioned dork.

~Will

[my heart melts]

I write back to him with a string of questions and he responds immediately:

Subject: RE: hey...

Originally I was born in Canada. But I was like 0.75 years old when we moved to California, so I'm pretty much Californian. But I was primarily raised in Nor Cal. I came to So Cal for school/career. I moved to Woodland Hills to have a nicer situation than living in Hollywood. Yeah, the plan is to write scripts professionally as opposed to working 12 hours then trying to do it.

I try to write as much as possible. I'm pretty much always doing research, keeping an online journal, writing an outline, working on a short, feature, or tv script.

How about you? What kind of design are you into? Architecture? What brings you to West Hills? I haven't seen too many hills there, have you? Then again, I haven't seen too many woodlands or hills in my area.

~Will

WHAT? He lives just MILES from me. I could really use a GOOD guy friend in the neighborhood...

I suggest "Woodlands Will" and I meet for coffee after work. He agrees.

On the way I stop for gas. As I reach into the pocket of my navy pea-coat for my wallet, my hand falls on a ticket. A ticket to the planetarium show, to be exact. My hand falls on the ticket... my mind falls to...

Laughing Lucas.

I arrive at Starbucks early and wait for Woodlands Will. As he pushes the glass door open and walks inside, I note that he looks younger than in his photos. His brown hair is parted to one side, and his mouth naturally falls into a hint of a smile. When I speak, he leans forwards, listening. He's down to earth and easygoing.

After we part ways, I try to determine if there's any chemistry and I can't decide. But, I feel relaxed in his company. I know I'd enjoy hanging out with him again but wonder if he'd even be interested in being my friend if I decide we can't be anything more than that? I don't have any friends close by in "the Woodlands." He would fill a major void. Is this Match.com abuse? Is it exclusively for finding boyfriends? What about platonic friends? Can I shop for those too?

I realize that I've embarked on this Match.com journey with the same mentality that I've had in order to survive the endless interviews that comprise a job search in the midst of a total-crap economy. I see it as a numbers game, where chances are it won't work out because so far, it hasn't. It hasn't seemed to matter that I graduated with honors, have a stellar portfolio, a ridiculous work ethic, or even that I THRIVE in interview situations. None of that matters, as proven by the fact that it hasn't worked out. Yes, I've found a part-time architecture gig in the most difficult job marketplace that our country has seen in decades. But, I had hoped that by now I'd have a full-time, nine to five, salaried job. I thought I'd have found "THE JOB." I note how hauntingly similar that sounds to finding "THE BOYFRIEND."

So, it only makes sense to set up as many "potential opportunities" as possible, right? But... the difference here is that this isn't about a job. It's about people and life, and these people that are "interviewing me" have the potential to be hurt. I'm not afraid of getting hurt, there's no crime in that. I'm worried about doing the hurting. I don't want to lead them on while poking around for other options, but... I don't want to cheat myself.

I want to know what's out there.

And I'm not in too much of a hurry. It's not like I see marriage in my near future, nor do I want to have children anytime soon. My younger sister on the other hand, can't wait to be a Mom. However, I'm currently SO anti-baby-making that I figure if, in the near future, I find myself in the mood to hang out with a screaming baby I can just play "library" with my sister, and temporarily check one of hers out.

At present, there aren't even convenient places in my life in which to fit a baby. Even at the Los Angeles Department of Building and Safety (where I'm often sent to attain building permits) the ledges in the women's' restrooms warn, "This is a plan holder not a baby changing table."

Have I proven my point? Me + marriage + babies = NOT on the near horizon. Not even yet in this SOLAR SYSTEM.

I realize I'm not paying attention to where I'm going and accidentally hop the curb. I glance in my rearview mirror and notice that Woodlands Will is following me out of the Starbucks parking lot.

Damn.

I call him and say:

"Please don't follow me as this is not an exit. I thought it was sloped down to the street. BIG shocker, it's not!"

(Embarrassing.)

When I get home, I put on my sweats, climb into bed with my laptop, and grudgingly prepare to sift through the continuously overwhelming number of messages waiting for me in my Match-box.

I find one from Motivated Mark, a 29-year-old who's (very successfully) into real estate private equity.

His profile reads:

I am a highly ambitious and hard working professional seeking a woman who's just as driven and go-getting! I'm looking for a woman who isn't afraid of a challenge or to set her sights high- yet a woman who can also find contentment in the here and now. Intelligence and a true connection are important. I think life is thrilling and strive to live it to the fullest.

Sounds promising, but I'm getting a bit tired from all these dates. Really. Yet, I'm curious, so I propose a date for tomorrow in Studio City. After he writes back to confirm, I shut off my laptop, return it to my desk, and get back in bed.

I pick up my phone to silence it for the night and notice a missed call and voicemail. It's from Older Oliver. He wants to know if I want to grab dinner sometime soon. Yes, I do... but is it a crime if I plan to have dinner with someone else the next night?

Maybe I'm getting in over my head.

Tuesday, January 26

100 MATCH DATES?!

I just got back from a FANTASTIC run. I have to admit, since embarking on this Match.com adventure I have had the most EXPLOSIVE workouts of my life. Apparently if I'm excited about something, it's evident in all aspects of my daily routine.

Drenched in sweat, I sit down on the carpet to stretch. I think of Older Oliver. I wonder if meeting me has added so much excitement to his life that it's manifested in everything he does. Is he feeling extra confident at work this week? Is he smiling more? If I were to screen his calls from here on out, would he be angry... or glad he met me? Could he take anything from our single hour together?

If I had messaged him on Match saying I was up for one coffee date, but nothing more than just one hour of interesting conversation with an interesting person, what would he have said?

I try to objectively critique what I am doing.

My intentions are good, but the aftermath could be bad.

I consider: if a random woman drives her grandmother to the hospital (talk about a flawless/pristine intention) and accidentally hits a pedestrian (causes harm), that well-intentioned granddaughter would still have to live with the fact that she caused injury. So, even if I AM looking to meet a "Match," what if people are hurt in the process?

I imagine this story as a movie. I feel nauseous when I realize the ending could be one of those cliché scripts that ends with all the men finding out that they were part of a "quest" of some sort, are furious, but ultimately understand. Ugh. Barf.

But, what if the "movie" ends with me as alone as when I started, but better in touch with myself? What if searching for a man helps me find myself? What if continuously refining my "profile" and introducing myself to strangers illuminates parts of my personality with which I had lost touch? I certainly hope I am helping these men learn something about themselves as well.

It's strange to think that sometimes it takes someone else to teach us something about our selves. I think this relates to what Older Oliver was saying about the short girls who say they'll only consider men over six feet tall. It's about us perhaps not KNOWING what we want.

For example:

I received the following message:

Subject: Your Smile (!)

You have the most beautiful smile. Your smile makes me smile, even tonight. I worked the night shift at the emergency room and it was a LONG shift. By the time I got home I was NOT in the best mood, but, I saw your smile, and I smiled. Please let me take you out to dinner.

Greg

ps. thanks for the smile

I check out his profile, and sincerely don't think I could be with him. I just don't.

Yet, I feel obliged to write back.

I respond:

Subject: RE: Your Smile (!)

Your message made my week, or possibly month but I don't think we're a good Match and I've recently met someone here and would like to see where it goes.

But... thank you.

I hope it's ok for me to print out what you wrote to keep for "rough" days... just as kind words from a total stranger...just that my smile made someone else smile. That alone makes me smile.

Best best wishes to you.

Rachel

Ok so... really I've met five people on Match and would like to see where it goes. I don't want to drag him into the mess I am potentially creating if I don't think he has a chance.

So, really, which is the less reckless route?

Perhaps the speed at which I jumped into Match.com was reckless. But... I can't say I regret any of it. A week ago I had zero men on the horizon. Now, I suppose you could say I'm dating between five and eight...

Talk about fast.

And, there's no hint of things slowing down.

I transition from my Match-box to my personal email inbox and find a job offer from the LA office of a renowned international firm. Apparently my interview from that day that I first met Paper-Perfect Peter DID go as well as I thought. Or maybe not because there's a catch: it's a horrific commute (into the heart of downtown) AND it's ten-hour workdays, five days a week, for three months... without compensation. I'm distraught and irritated. I forward it to my aunt Thea, a ridiculously successful NYC executive who is my most valued advisor and constant cheerleader on my JOB SEARCH.

She always has her "crack-berry" (as my Dad likes to call it) on her, so she responds promptly:

Rachel -

Congratulations on the offer!

Can we schedule a call to discuss "live"?

We need an action plan that gets you asap to Phase #2:

- full-time compensated job with an architecture firm

- that is hot stuff in design

- and certified in CA

- and has a workable commute

When is good for you to talk? And dare I mention coming to work in NYC? (Aren't you proud of me, I didn't mention it for all of 2009?)

Love, Aunt Thea

Ok, so I don't have a job that is "full time" (I typically log 20 hours per week at the architecture office) with "workable commute" (the trip takes an hour and a half, minimum) but I DO have MULTIPLE men that keep me busy "full time," are "hot stuff," and all within twenty miles of LA ("workable commute")!

On the way to my date with Motivated Mark, I call aunt Thea. "So," she asks, "what's the news that's fit to print?!"

Honestly, not much has happened on the job front since our last pow-wow, but I talk her ear off for about an hour about Match.com and how it has turned my life upside down. After I hang up, I realize maybe this Internet love-quest is just a distraction. Maybe it's a way for me to feel like I'm making progress and moving forward here in California. I haven't gotten the job, but I am getting the guy... or guys. At least in one sense I'm achieving a bit of success. When the economy inconveniently plummeted as I prepared to graduate and enter the job market, aunt Thea was the one who reminded me, "When life throws you lemons, make lemonade."

So, when I could only secure part-time/project-based work, I made GLOW IN THE DARK HOT PINK LEMONADE by investing in myself (by starting a small design company which ultimately led to few gigs including the graphic design for a book cover, development of two patterns for a new line of eco-chic fabrics, and a large pro-bono but high-profile interior design project). I realized the NEON lemonade would take time to sweeten, so I simultaneously began brewing a not-as-impressive batch of BLAND, UNINSPIRING, YET THIRST QUENCHING LEMONADE, by working as a computer tutor on the weekends. No, "computer tutor" does not sound as exciting as "design firm, founding partner," but my car always seems to be thirsty and doesn't seem to care which type of lemonade I make, as long as I keep the tank full.

And now, I've added a new batch of lemonade: Match-ade, which is perhaps the quirkiest yet most fruitful concoction yet...

I pull into the Studio City Shopping Center parking garage and realize I'm not wearing any makeup and haven't really looked in a mirror yet today. I ravage through my purse and find an old tube of mascara. Geez. With so many dates, I'm getting sloppy.

When I approach the cafe I can see Motivated Mark through the windows. He has good posture, is handsome, and is wearing... a sweater vest (super-cute!).

He stands up and I extend my hand for a shake, but he motions for a hug. We sit down and I am conscious of the fact that he is delicately standing on that fine line between boy and man. He is definitely a man, but just barely... because there is something youthful about him. I'm confused. Is he is a man that has a boyish face or a boy with a mature demeanor? Considering he's 29, I settle on the former.

I explain, "I'm having one of those days where it's 2pm and I feel like I've already had an entire day. That much has happened. Do you ever have those?"

"Yes, absolutely."

(God he's handsome.)

We talk about our jobs, California, commuting... We talk quickly. It all feels a bit rushed, but perhaps that's because we are both busy energetic professionals. We're used to functioning with our default set to "high efficiency" mode. There are no silences between sentences and when he pauses there is barely a second before I jump in... and vise versa.

It's all a bit tiring.

I suggest we get up and order our beverages. He didn't hear me order, and asks which tea I chose.

"Orange infused green tea, hot," I say.

"Oh, I've had that one, it's horrific," he says, a little too loud for my liking.

The barista grins.

"Thanks," I say sarcastically.

We sit down and jump back in to fast-paced conversation. "So how long have you been on Match?" I ask.

"On and off for seven years, I've had long term relationships in between and so there have been long periods where I've withdrawn from it."

"Oh, wow, and how many women have you actually met face to face?" I ask.

He replies, "Probably about one-hundred."

"OH, wow..."

"Shocked?" he asks.

(No, I'm not shocked, just a little surprised, and excited. Finally, a guy that I can be completely transparent with and fully lay my cards on the table.)

"I've been on the site eight days and have been on six dates, including this one."

We both laugh, loudly.

I anxiously attempt to taste my tea, and burn my tongue.

According to Motivated Mark, I shouldn't feel guilty about ignoring messages from men I'm not interested in. It's expected. Men have a "shot gun" approach to online dating. They only expect responses from one out of every five women they reach out to, if that. And this is coming from a highly "eligible bachelor."

"There are thousands of people on Match.com that are single, and don't want to be," he states.

"That's pretty miserable!" I exclaim.

"Well, there are so many people to choose from, all 'within thirty miles of Los Angeles, California' (as Match would say), that everyone is looking for their 'ideal'. The mentality is, why put up with ANYTHING that isn't ideal when there are so many fish in THIS sea," he says.

I respond, "It's interesting you say that, because to be honest, I have met really great men this week through Match.com. And in any other situation, only one of them would be in my life at a time. So, I'd be dating them… or rather 'him'. For sure. He would be the only option on the horizon, and the truth would be that my life would be more fun with him than without him. It's fascinating that I don't 'settle' in any facet of my life except with relationships. I've definitely dated 'good guys' that I was lukewarm about. But now that there are so many guys on the horizon that have been 'pre-screened' to match all of my "make or break" criteria… well… I have a 'don't settle for anything less than ideal' mentality. Because I don't have to. I get an overwhelming number of messages from seemingly genuine, intelligent, energetic men and I would probably enjoy the companionship of any of them. But now my standards are rising, because there are so many to choose from. The sick thing at this point is that when I get a message, rather than looking to see the best in this potential companion- I am looking for 'the flaw'. I have to approach every message with an incredibly critical eye, so that I can 'delete' the message and clear out the Match-box. I don't have time to 'waste' on those that I wouldn't actually meet because it's taking time from responding to those that I actually would."

He jumps in, "Well that makes sense. And it's ok because like I said, the men don't expect responses. I have a roommate who is on Match and she gets an overwhelming number of responses from creeps. She also meets some really great guys, but decides not to pursue them because they're 'lacking' in one way or another… perhaps they have a dead end job, or no job… Even I've meet some exciting, smart, sexy women, and have found myself looking for better because THEY have a dead end job."

(I wonder what he will think of my multiple "jobs", or if my many "half jobs" make one big super "whole job"…)

And now I interject, "Well, it's because you won't settle for less than your ideal. Because in this society we were raised to believe we can have whatever we want. You want the whole package. With so many choices, you have confidence it's out there. Or she's out there."

"Exactly" he says. "And, in LA, everyone has their shit together. Event the fat girls have their shit together. There are two curvy women at my office and boy are they sexy. Well dressed, fashionable, they have it together. When I go back home to Montana I find myself looking around in dismay at how the majority of people dress, and I bet they are looking at my like I'm a pretty boy/girly man."

(This first of his remarks that rubs me the wrong way… the REALLY wrong way. "Even the fat girls have their shit together." So offensive, but I try not to discount him just yet…perhaps he's just nervous and didn't mean what he just said.)

I re-attempt the tea. He was right, it tastes like crap.

I change the subject. I want to take advantage of how openly and comfortably we seem to be discussing this whole Match.com thing. I ask, "so, what do you think about making friends through Match? I have met some incredible men and even though I may not have chemistry with them, I'd like to be able to be friends with them. But, I worry that because they're on Match.com they have tunnel vision and are focused on finding a girlfriend, and have an all or nothing mentality about it."

He pauses, "well, I think it depends on the guy. If he's been here for a long time, he probably has more than enough friends. If he's new to town, or a recent transplant, he might be open to that."

I respond, "I just think that chemistry is such a funny thing. Either you have it or you don't. And even if you don't, the way I see it, if we still obviously have a lot in common why not be friends?"

The conversation continues for just under two hours. Motivated Mark looks at his watch and says, "Sorry, but I really need to get back to work."

He is the first of my dates to end it. Usually, I'm the time keeper.

As we prepare to part ways at the parking garage he says, "I would definitely like to see you again."

"Me too," I reply (although I'm still a bit unsettled about his "fat girls" remark and hope it was just caused by first-date jitters).

"I'll call you later in the week," he says.

"My parents will be in town visiting all week, so next week is more realistic," I say.

"Okay then!" he says.

I flash him a big smile and then turn to leave.

I realize I don't have the foggiest idea where I parked.

Dammit.

As soon as I get home I make a bee-line for my laptop. I have to get this all in writing before it fades.

Next, I check my Match-box and find, you guessed it, MORE emails from Match-men.

The most notable, is from a very handsome, 32-year-old, who closely resembles Mathew Broderick (think "Ferris Bueller's Day Off"), who I not-so-foundly refer to as "COCKY CONNOR." Connor is a professional pilot turned very successful salesman (for an aircraft manufacturer). WHY do I refer to him as "COCKY CONNER?!" Well, let me catch you up to speed with my correspondence with him thus far…

Within six hours of me joining Match, he wrote:

Subject: Hey good lookin!

How was your weekend? Do anything fun?

My weekend was AWESOME. Last week I hit my sales goals out of the park, ordered all new high-performance water-ski equipment, and made plans to take a weekend trip with my buddies.

Connor

I responded:

RE: Hey good lookin!

Thank you for your message. There was nothing personal in it though, so I have to wonder if you sent it to many Match.com ladies!

To be perfectly honest, I find you very attractive and smiled through reading your profile HOWEVER:

1. I'm 24, and worry we may be in slightly different places in life (due to the age gap)

and

2. I don't like to ski (neither on land or in water), although, I do like to layout on boats while others ski and LOVE to roast marshmellows and relax by a fire...

So there you have it.

Cheers,

Rachel

I know, I'm a ball-buster. But, please have sympathy; this was before my "dates" explained the whole Match.com/shot gun approach from their perspective! I wrote to him during my pre-Older Oliver/Motivated Mark days! And, incredibly enough, he had the guts to reply to my blunt message:

RE: RE: Good morning!

You are right; my email to you was not personal in the slightest. However, since I really don't know you yet, I really didn't know what to say! I do know me though, so I guess I choose to mention what I do know in hopes of saying something of interest to you.

You are right again about our age difference. However, I have had good experiences with women both above and below my age. You're a bit younger than what I'm looking for but you seem mature and I'm intrigued. I say it's worth a shot- even if you don't like to ski. I'm just as happy to relax on a boat and cuddle by a fire.

Hope I didn't scare you off.

Connor

Ps. Please email me back at my personal email account (not through Match)- COnnorCO101@gmail.com.

I have learned that "email me through my personal email account" really means "I'm embarrassed to be seen on Match.com by my co-workers."

Ok, back to responding to Connor:

Connor,

Please let me apologize for my blunt email. I received your message within the first 24 hours of joining "Match.com" and I didn't fully understand it from the "male perspective." At this point, I'm certainly NO expert- but have been on a few dates and have had a few very interesting and revealing discussions. From my experience, women get bombarded with messages, while men expect to receive responses from about 1/5 of those they reach out to. I'm not sure if that is accurate, but it's what I've been told. I can therefore understand why men are reluctant to invest the time in crafting personalized messages, when, unfortunately (?) most women blatantly ignore them.

Also, when I began this "Match.com adventure" my intended "age bracket" was set in stone. I had never dated anyone more than two years my senior. However, after actually going on a date with a 30-year-old, I truly found myself more attracted to and more intrigued by these men than I have yet been by those my exact age. So I'm now much more open to it. This has been a great experience. In learning about other people I am learning about myself in unexpected ways. And it's only been about a week!

Now, to respond to your questions:

Re: different places in life: There are plenty of "external"/objective ways to describe me. Whether it's by my age, job, interests, or achievements- but those are not things that I would want the person I'm dating to value me for. Yes appreciate, but it's not the focus of a relationship. So you're right, those things aren't too important.

Glad my disinterest in skiing is not a deal breaker.

I do find a good fire mesmerizing. When I lived in Switzerland there was a fire in the hearth (which was about six feet wide, truly incredible) almost every evening. I would sit in a chair with my feet warming (so much so that one night the soles of my flats began to get soft and melt) and read. I also love the smell of orange peels in the fire. Have you ever peeled an orange and then tossed the peels into the flames? It smells like citrus... and warmth... and holiday. That is the only way I can describe it. My dad always threw his orange peels in the fire, so perhaps the scent simply makes me sentimental- and when I was in a foreign country it reminded me of home.

I love the feel of the sun on my skin, so yes- being on a boat is something I enjoy. I love love love to be warm. Some people don't like to feel "too hot." For me, there's no such thing! I love the heat. I did move from the DC area to the LA area after all, didn't I?!

My weekend was relaxing. I spent Sunday at the Spa in Santa Monica with a best friend of mine. Told her all about Match.com. I may have created a new "Match convert."

Meet for coffee one day soon? I don't like to spend too much of my life on the Internet...

Cheers,

Rachel

It's 11pm. I climb into bed... and can't sleep. I feel a bit queasy, tense, and restless. Of the men I have met so far, I don't know which I prefer the most. It bothers me. I want to see them again to decide, but that could be leading them on. It eats at me.

I hope they are also dating more than one person. I know, weird.

I rack my brain for flaws in each of them. I review our dates looking for red flags to eliminate a few of them and narrow it down. This mindset bothers me. The whole thing bothers me. I spend the night squirming in uncomfortable thoughts.

THIS IS NOT FICTION BECAUSE I AM NOT A "WRITER." IF YOU THINK I COULD MAKE THIS ALL UP, YOU ARE WRONG.

I have a passion for building places, not plots. I want to hone the craft of creating spaces, not stories. I never intended to write a book, just keep a journal (per Tess's encouragement). These chapters are merely my notes typed up and formatted as only an anal design obsessive could. I am having a field day with the formatting decisions. Yes, I know, the margins are pretty perfect, thank you very much.

At this point, I feel truly indebted to Tess. The guys are starting to blend together a bit and I'm starting to have déjà vu during dates. It's hard to keep track of what I've said to whom. These words are a wonderful resource for me when I'm trying to remember. This is my study guide so that I can mentally place any man in the correct context. Keeping up with Match.com could be a full-time job.

At 8 am I drive to Santa Monica to meet with Lucille, one of my computer tutees. On the way, I fret about juggling my various "suitors." I even attempt to jot a few notes down on a napkin (the only thing I have within reach on which to write) while swerving through Topanga Canyon. If you know Topanga you know this is lethal. If you don't know Topanga, please don't Google it, because it might leave you feeling obligated to call my parents and tattle on me. Actually, I hesitate to write this in case there is a loophole that would allow the LAPD to retroactively issue me a reckless driving ticket.

I have my car radio set to NPR. As experts weigh in on "the contested election in Sri Lanka" and discuss "the possibility of Yemen becoming the next Afghanistan and producing terrorists," the logical part of me says GET A GRIP, RACHEL. There are more important things to fret about.

I turn up NPR and tune OUT any Match.com thoughts.

As always, the first thing I do at Lucille's condo is remove my shoes (routine). Next, I put my lunch in her fridge, sit down in the chair beside her, and say "good morning" (routine).

"Well, what's new?" she asks (routine).

"I've been on five dates in the past week and pretty soon I think I'll be dating nine guys… at once," I reply (NOT routine).

Lucille stares at me blankly, then proceeds to laugh hysterically for a good 35 seconds. Lucille broke two of her ribs last week and experiences severe pain while breathing and walking. Thirty-five seconds of rib-cage-shaking hilarity must mean that what I said was fairly funny.

I wait until she regains her composure.

"What's so funny?" I ask.

"Well… this coming from YOU… who had NO dates… who hardly had a social life!" she says.

"Well, thanks!" I remark.

At one point Lucille asked me if I was a lesbian because I literally never mentioned any men in my life. I explained that honestly I'm a private person. She's a client, and I like to keep our relationship professional, and, well, there just really ARENT a lot of men in my life! It was apparent to me, but I didn't know it was also apparent to my clients?!

I tell her I'm considering writing a book about it. She said she'd read it if she could tolerate the rib pain.

"Can I put you and your reaction in my book?"

She replies, "The only place I don't like to be put is in my place." Now we're back to "typical."

After tutoring Lucille, I swing by my house to pick up my 16-year-old sister and parents who are visiting from Virginia. We drive to the Getty Villa and, not surprisingly, I attempt to enter through the "exit ONLY" gate. The security guard approaches my window, and I ask him for directions to the proper entrance. He's cute.

Apparently my mother thinks so too.

"Are you on Match.com?" she calls out from the back seat.

My sister and I burst out laughing.

I locate the proper entrance and the same security guard greets us.

"Parking is fifteen dollars, right?" I ask, as Dad passes me a twenty.

"Free!" he says with a smile.

I reply, "But I thought…"

"Free for you," he says, with a wink.

It's official: Match.com brings good luck ☺.

As we leave the parking lot, I postulate (out loud) that if this is a bit of a scientific experiment, there should only be one variable (the guy) and everything else must remain constant (me, the location, the time, and what I'm wearing) in order for me to make any logical hypotheses about which guy is the one for me.

But I worry that soon my answers will sound rehearsed. I will begin to come off as unauthentic. It's a legitimate fear.

I confess another concern to my mother. I worry that when these men discover I'm writing a book, they'll discount anything I may have said to them. They might question whether my words or actions were an act or a stunt for the book. She reminds me, "But, sweetie, you didn't start this to write a book. You started this to find someone. The book idea came after you began the journey."

She's right, but the men don't know that. And they might get angry or storm off without giving me the chance to explain.

Dad has walked ahead, and we hurry down the stairs of the amphitheater to catch up.

The grounds of the Getty are beautiful. The architecture is stunning and unforgettable. That is what I'm looking to find on one of these dates: unforgettable. I want to feel inspired. I want to have chemistry with a man in the way that I have chemistry with buildings. I want to find a man who enchants me in the way that Peter Zumthor's thermal baths in Vals did. When I visited that building I wanted to stay all day. Even if I had had the night there too, it would not have been enough to satiate my hunger to know those spaces. I waded in the interior pools for hours, entranced by the reflections of the water on the cavernous walls. I had to touch, to run my hand along the concrete. I want to find a man who makes me want to stay all day. I want to find a man with whom one night would not be enough to satiate my hunger to know him and his body. Who makes me want to learn every cave of his mind, to experience a magnetic force that compels me to run my hand along the crevices and texture of his face the way the stone walls called to my fingertips in Vals.

I knew within three seconds of entering the Museé d'Orsay that it was love at first sight. I believe in love at first sight. Perhaps you're thinking that it's impossible to have love for a building, buildings don't communicate. I beg to differ.

They speak to me. That museum swept me off my feet. I want to find a man capable of doing the same.

The villa is so lovely that meandering through the courtyards makes anything seem possible. I want to return, soon.

When I get home, I message Older Oliver to see if he's interested in meeting me at the Getty Villa on Friday. We decide instead to rendezvous at the Villa's "sister," the Getty Center, for lunch and an architecture tour. Speaking with him reminds me how different his voice is from my previous boyfriends', much deeper.

Later, he sends a message asking:

Would you like me to pick you up? I assume (based on what you told me about your personal safety precautions) that you prefer to drive separately. Either is fine with me ;).

Hahaha, he's funny. And it appears he finds me funny—or maybe just insane. Either is amusing. Do I really come off as such a safety psycho? Again, I am learning about myself and how others perceive me.

I note the messages piling up in my Match-box but decide to take a break for the time being. After all, I'm a human being, not a serial dater.

I take a shower, put on a dress I know my mother AND grandmother will like, and join everyone downstairs where my aunt and uncle are throwing a family dinner party for Grandpa Sam's birthday. No one in the California branch of my family is shy, especially my cousin Kate (recall her "Internet slut" remark). I still recall (with humiliation) the year that I started to "develop" and, on seeing me at the airport, she LOUDLY acknowledged it. She shouted something along the lines of "OOOOOOO, RACHEL HAS LITTLE BOOBIES!" I'm fairly certain she proceeded to grab at them. I was twelve. At age twelve, even tripping when NO ONE IS AROUND is completely and unbearably mortifying. The fact that the entire airport was now aware of the contents of my training bra—well, "shoot me now" doesn't even come close to the string of thoughts I suffered following her public display.

If I want real, uncensored reactions to my crazy quest, tonight's dinner table is it.

I explain what I've been up to, mention the people I've met, and open the floor for discussion.

Uncle Carl begins. "Little one, you have to be prepared for Connor to invite you to join the Mile High Club. Do you know what that is?"

My dad leaves the table to get more water. Or to get a shotgun to be ready for Connor.

Grandma Rose brings up the fact that I've met someone who looks like uncle Jake.

"He looks like Nicolas Cage, he acts like uncle Jake, and he's VERY handsome," I say.

"Yes, he is handsome," Mom agrees. (Let me make a point of mentioning, here, that NO ONE at this table has met ANY of these men. But, all of the women at the table have all watched over my shoulder as I've logged into Match.com. Therefore they ALL have opinions. LOTS of them.) Mom continues, "I'm having trouble keeping them all straight."

"YOU'RE having trouble? I'M having trouble. I've resorted to using a BINDER. Before getting out of the car for each date, I do a quick profile review," I say.

The entire table finds this very, very funny. I thought it was just plain logical. Grandma Rose wants to know if, given the number of men I'm currently "getting to know," am I considering put a halt on "new additions."

"No," I say. "I've met some great guys, but none of them has totally 'knocked my socks off'. Why should I stop looking when there could be a 'love at first sight' guy out there for me?"

"Maybe it doesn't happen like that," aunt Ellen says.

"For me, it can. I know it can, because I've experienced it before," I say.

"And what happened?" cousin Kate asks.

"We were best friends, we dated for a while, and then it ended."

"So even when you thought you found love at first sight, it didn't work out?" she questions. "Maybe you were wrong."

"I don't think I was wrong. Just because it didn't last doesn't mean we weren't in love. We WERE in love. You know when you meet someone and you just know they're the type of person you want to spend every waking moment with? The type of person you want to spend every sleeping moment with too... because... you love them. The feeling that every day all day with them... isn't enough. When I was in love, I was so happy. I would never wish that undone. No matter how unhappy I was when it ended. I want to find that sort of happiness again," I explain.

My mom speaks up, "But I thought he broke your heart."

"Maybe so, but it was I who gave it to him to break and maybe I broke his too."

"But when you started dating him you were so sure it was right..."

"I learned from it. I learned that two greats don't always make a grand... that sometimes they make a mess."

"And you really don't regret it?"

(I can tell she's been waiting for a chance to ask me these questions, and I notice the rest of the table has fallen silent. Fourteen pairs of eyes are watching my mother and me as if we are separated from the rest of the dinner guests and on display in a glowing, glass fish tank.)

I reply, "No. I don't regret it. I can't regret it. I could never regret learning my heart's capacity for delight, even if it came at the cost of learning its intolerance for pain."

My mother smiles, one of those quiet smiles that hints of both sadness and understanding. She's sad I've been hurt, yet she understands why I feel it was worth it. And perhaps she's proud that I'm willing to risk being hurt in order to grow.

I continue, "I can't predict from a piece of paper or an Internet screen if I'll have chemistry or love at first sight with someone before we meet. All of the men I do agree to meet satisfy my criteria. They are screened; they pass all my tests except the chemistry test. So really, it's a numbers game. I want to meet as many of these men as possible, and hopefully, with one of them I'll sense sparks."

"So, no sparks yet?" Grandma Rose asks.

The fish tank shatters and I swim out and back onto the table.

"Well, I'm not sure," I say.

"She wanted to tell Oliver she wasn't sure what she thought or where she saw it going after the first date! Men don't want to hear that! " My mom exclaims.

"When your uncle Fred told me he loved me and wanted to marry me, I told him I wasn't sure," says cousin Kate, "and then, a few months later I told him I was sure, and he said, well, now, HE wasn't! That made me REALLY sure!" She laughs.

"I always wondered what made you come around," my mom says.

I put the focus back on me by asking, "So I don't have to know on the first date? And I can just say that I'd like to see that person again even if I'm not sure what could come of it?"

"You're not expected to be sure after a first date," my uncle Dave says. "A first date is like your first screening into medical school (he's a doctor). A second date just means that you didn't do anything so offensive on the first date/first interview that you've been completely scratched off the list."

My mom turns to uncle Dave and asks, "How many of your long-term relationships were love at first sight?"

He says, "Well, men and women are different. I think that women fall slower. Men are a little bit more visually instinctive; they are more likely to be interested right away. Then a woman would have to do something awful to turn them off. Women, I think, are the opposite. They keep an open mind, but they don't fall. And then at some point they do fall, but it takes a while."

So there I have it. The prescription for making (and breaking) the love potion, straight from the doctor's mouth. It's almost as crystal clear and easy to follow as when my father asked aunt Thea, "What advice can you give about the stock market?" and she responded with wisdom: "Don't buy dumb stocks."

My mom interjects, "Men don't want to hear that you haven't fallen yet!"

"RIGHT," says uncle Dave.

"They want to hear 'let's go out again'?" I ask.

"Right," he says.

"I just worry it will take a few dates with someone for me to realize that I DON'T want to go out again. Then I'll break it off and it will seem totally from left field."

Uncle Dave says, "Well, it's different with different people. I've had girls where I knew right when I met them, and others where it took a bit longer. With some women, we were friends first, and I knew them strictly as friends, and then later I was able to see what was right in front of me."

Aunt Ellen chimes in again, "Sometimes it takes longer!"

"But maybe I don't want to go on a second date with someone, thinking well, it wasn't GREAT, but I if I stick with it someday it might be. Especially when I've LIVED the scenario where GREATNESS is apparent at first sight."

Aunt Ellen says, "That's not realistic, that's Hollywood."

I argue, "But it IS realistic, I've lived it!"

Aunt Ellen says, "What about those speed dating events? Maybe you need to go to one of those."

"Those are Match.com without the profiles. Those are ONLY about chemistry and nothing else because you form your judgment within a few minutes of meeting someone. BEFORE you can know what you might have in common," I say.

"But you are meeting these people in non-social situations. You aren't meeting them at a party; you're sbasically interviewing them over a cup of coffee. Don't you think that's a lot of pressure?" my mom asks.

"Let me tell you what you are doing now" my dad says. "You are dating by committee."

And then, out of nowhere, uncle Dave divulges, "I met my wife on Match.com."

WHAT?! And he's JUST bringing this up NOW?!

After dinner I retreat to my room and find an email from Cocky Connor, the 32-year-old I probably initially offended but later reneged my obnoxious message.

It reads:

Hi Rachel,

Thanks for the reply— and no need to apologize. I always appreciate honesty, even bluntness! Further, I think it's awesome that your experiences on Match have opened you up to dating men slightly above your age. Up for coffee this weekend?

Connor

I reply, suggesting we meet Sunday.

ROMEO, JULIET, AND THE MICROSCOPIC LINE BETWEEN ROMANTIC AND CORNY

I arrive at the architecture office and discuss my latest Match.com adventures with a colleague. I actually manage to survive undistracted until 3:21 pm before giving in and checking my Match-box. There's a message from Adventure Alex. It's been there for over 24 hours, but I've just been feeling too overwhelmed to sift through it all (current Match-box total = 80 messages). I'm starting to think of it as one of those washing machines with too much soap in it... the kind in the cartoons that ultimately explodes in a sudsy mess. I take a deep breath and plunge into the message:

Subject: RE: and you thought the 1st was long...

Hey Rachel.

Reading your messages has been great. A bit of a break from the hustle-bustle around here. Please feel free to keep them coming. I think we will ultimately need to meet each other to see if there's a real "spark" (I would definitely love to get together when I get back), but there's no harm in getting to know you a little better beforehand.

Oh, Kenya. Well, my best friend from college is out here doing development work for a nonprofit. He took a year off medical school at Stanford to work with these guys so I knew their project was special. I did some work for his team remotely (compiled a database, made some maps, etc.) that turned out to be really helpful to the project, so his boss invited me to check out the site and train some of their workers in GPS data collection and the like. I'm only here for the rest of the week, but it's been amazing so far.

So you lived in Switzerland? Where else have your travels taken you?

If you liked the word "nifty," you're really going to enjoy our conversations.

Okay. You were very perceptive in noticing that I didn't speak too much about my appreciation for art. Let me address that and please... bear with me.

I've spent hours wandering the Louvre in Paris. I dragged my sister back and forth between the Galleria di Uffizi and the Galleria dell'Accademia in Florence. I sought out the Rembrandt museum and the Van Gogh museum by myself in Amsterdam. I took in the walls and ceilings of the Vatican in Rome. I spent an entire day lost in the British Museum.

I've toured the Met, MOMA, Natural History Museum and the Guggenheim in New York City. I've seen Stonehenge on the Salisbury plane of Wiltshire, England, had lunch at the Château de Chenonceau on the River Cher in the Loire Valley, and kissed the Blarney Stone at Blarney Castle outside Cork, Ireland.

I toured the Bob Marley museum (and later visited his grave) in Jamaica. I attended a performance of A Midsummer Night's Dream in Shakespeare's own Globe Theatre in London. I saw an amazing cast perform Rossini's Barber of Seville at the LA Opera and saw the LA Phil perform Handel's Messiah just across the street. I've seen numerous productions on Broadway and even caught Wicked before it left the Pantages.

I take everyone who visits me in LA to the Getty (even if it's just hanging out on the patio) and watched the reconstruction of the Getty Villa in anticipation of its opening. I have been to every museum on Wilshire Boulevard in LA (including the Page Museum at the La Brea Tar Pits) several times as well as the Museum of Tolerance and the Museum of Jurassic Technology (you know where those are if you're a real LA dweller) ☺.

Okay, now, if you've made it this far, you get the truth. I am just not a huge fan of art. Obviously I've tried to give myself every opportunity to develop an appreciation, but it's just not my gig. I will always visit a museum if I have the opportunity (and even go out of my way to do so) because I have seen things that have taken my breath away, but by and large, I'm more impressed with feats of mechanical and structural engineering. I'm more impressed with the massive sequoias in northern California and the jagged peaks of the Rocky Mountains. I made fun of art majors in college (though I regret it now), and I don't have an artistic bone in my body.

There you have it. My confession. Hopefully this is not an irreconcilable, but I understand if it is.

How about you? Knowing what you know about me, any confessions? We might as well make this interesting :).

Talk soon,

Alex

I notice another message from him as well:

Subject: RE: and you thought the 1st was long...

Hey!

So I haven't heard from you.

I'm supposed to be the one in the jungle remember ☺?

Anyway, seriously, I hope my last email didn't come off the wrong way. You probably think I'm either arrogant for ranting about my "artistic encounters" or just narrow-minded for not being an art buff. I like to think I am neither.

Just in case you are not snubbing me and just haven't had a chance to write back, I hope you're having a wonderful week back in LA and I hope to hear from you soon. In fact, I hope that is the case regardless.

Cheers!

Alex

Ok, lots to say, here goes:

Alex,

I like that you said "I like to think I am neither" rather than "I don't like to think I'm either." There's a subtle (but revealing) difference.

I'm sorry it has taken me a while to respond. I have been very busy, my parents are in town (have not seen them since Thanksgiving and they are here for four days en route to Hawaii), AND my Match.com inbox is exploding and I was a bit fearful/putting off going through it (although I'm usually not a procrastinator). The volume is intimidating, especially since there are so many other things in my "real" (non-Internet) life that I want to be focusing on (family/work).

I don't snub. ☺ And I wasn't offended.

To each their own. My ONLY interest in YOUR harboring an interest in art is completely self-serving. IF you too, take pleasure in art, then we can spend time exploring art venues and it will be mutually enjoyable. I could continue to seek art venues and related events without feeling guilty or selfish for dragging someone to see something that only I cared to see. Do you know what I mean? For instance, if I met someone who LOVED spending months in Antarctica (I hate hate hate to be cold and love love love to be warm), I would have to either spend months being miserably cold or he would have to survive living "miserably" far from Antarctica. Extreme example, but I'm just illustrating the logic.

I suspect because I'm so young (so much I want to see and do apart from anyone else's desires), I am incredibly averse to sacrifice in a relationship. Compromise is important, but not sacrifice. But I would hope you wouldn't ask me to sacrifice my interest in art, just make compromises in certain situations. I don't have to do things that are EXCLUSIVELY art-related. And often such events in the more general sense are overarching, like the outdoor concerts at the Getty on Saturday nights. I might go to enjoy the art/ambiance while others could go exclusively for the music... or even the cocktails! Jean Nouvel's architecture drew me to the new concert hall in Lucerne, Switzerland, to hear the St. Petersburg Philharmonic—and I'll openly admit I was as touched by the music as by the building.

Besides, I can have fun OUTSIDE of an art museum. And I am in AWE of your valiant (can't think of a more perfect word) effort/search for "art appreciation." Maybe this might help: in order to appreciate a work of art you don't have to "like" it. You can understand how it is a manifestation of the time in which it was created, or that it is essential because it influenced or opened the door for later artistic movements, without "liking" it. Just an idea to consider.

And, honestly, there are some museums I adore more for their architecture than for their art.

I am a student of design, yet I have seen MANY artistic works that have left me emotionless and unfazed.

But, too: I have stood in L'Orangerie in Paris, where Monet's Lilies wrapped the walls, and was overwhelmed. I lost track of time and became oblivious to the presence of the other visitors. The beauty of the canvases was too real, the colors too vibrant. It was one of the most moving experiences of my entire life. So I too have seen things that have taken my breath away as well as those that have left me unmoved. Besides, I found the Louvre disappointing/frustrating. There were so many tourists that I felt like I was at an amusement park, not a sacred vault of art. If I could have a private tour... in the empty museum... now that could be incredible. But after reading The Da Vinci Code, it might also be terrifying, lol.

I visited galleries in Italy with my parents about five years ago, and just yesterday my mother and I were laughing as we recalled how we walked quickly past the enormous paintings of battle scenes (horror!), while my father and brother gaped in amazement at the illustrations of men gauging each other's eyes out.

Not irreconcilable.

Confessions? Hmmm... I suppose I should admit I'm not spontaneous. At all. I plan ahead. This doesn't seem like a deal-breaker but many men are looking for someone spontaneous. Random.

Let's continue these conversations in person... too much time on the Internet! I should be leaving work about now and you should be taking advantage of being in Kenya. Go explore!

Just let me know when you plan on returning and we can set up a day/time to meet.

Cheers,
Rachel

My correspondence with Adventure Alex is starting to seem, well, a bit over the top. Dramatic. Part of me thinks this is the most romantic week of my life. The other part wants to roll my eyes and brush this all off as corniness.

Internet dating sounds so high tech, but really, it's a return to traditional in many ways. Long letters back and forth, the man wooing the woman with words, sounds very… Shakespeare.

Archaic.

Further, the constant stream of men "winking" and then using their profiles to "strut their stuff" and illustrate their strengths is downright animalistic. I imagine a male peacock flaunting his feathers in an effort to catch the eye of the unfazed female. I recall a conversation I once had with my 21-year-old brother. He claimed that it is the "woman's responsibility" to "select" a man suitable to "seed" her children. He explained that men are wired to procreate and women are therefore obligated to "select" the men whose children she wishes to bear. Women play a key role in "survival of the fittest" by choosing the men they find the most "fit."

I imagine prehistoric women choosing the biggest, burliest men who "kill the most woolly mammoths." How does that translate today? Most techno gadgets? Largest income? Perhaps women who date men based on material qualities are perhaps those most in touch with their instinctual inclination to select the most "able" mate? Certainly in today's society exceptional muscles or a remarkable ability to bring home large mammals to roast is not a measure of success.

I have no expertise in prehistoric women, cavemen, or woolly mammoths, so I would recommend taking all of these random thoughts with a grain of salt. Or more than a grain of salt. Take these thoughts with the 3,621,083 gallons of water from the (polluted) yet super-salty Pacific Ocean.

Friday, January 29

RACHEL, MEET SOMETHING WE CALL A "CAP," THE SOLUTION TO ANY POTENTIALLY RECEDING HAIRLINES

I wake up at 6:45 am for an early workout with my dad. Living halfway between east and west coast time (with my parents visiting from Virginia) is starting to wear on me. I know this because I slept like a rock last night, regardless of the multiple-date-induced acid reflux that has plagued me the past few nights.

We drive to Will Rogers State Park for a father-daughter run. I'm excited to finally have some alone time with my dad. As we start up a mulched trail, I ask him what he thinks about my Match.com project.

I preface the question with a tirade of defensive sentences (explaining that I'm meeting individuals I would never have had the opportunity to meet otherwise). My consistently long-winded lawyer father replies with one word:

"Remarkable."

My dad believes in creating opportunities to meet new people, taking chances, keeping life FULL, and jumping from one activity to the next (without pausing a second to rest or catch his breath). He gets it.

And, my dad can see that this is bringing me joy, and he likes to see me happy. Earlier this week he proved how much he likes to see me happy by running an unpleasant and foreign errand. I had mentioned to my mother that I was running low on tampons but wouldn't have time to pick some up. If she passed a drugstore, would she mind stopping in for me? I have to assume my dad overheard the request or my mother didn't find the time and passed the request to him. Either way, Dad came through with an absurdly large box (80 tampons, to be exact) of every imaginable size. He obviously hadn't the foggiest idea what he was looking for so he played it safe (better safe than sorry), because he likes to keep me happy.

Running out of tampons midweek = very, very unhappy. However, now I don't think I will have to worry about running out of tampons midYEAR.

During the run, we pass a patch of pathetic trees roped behind a sign: "PLANT REHABILITATION ZONE. DO NOT DISTURB." I laugh out loud and say, "Dad, isn't it kinda funny that I'm seeking a quality guy in a city where even the PLANTS need rehab?"

Different geographic locations have different signs and breed different people. Am I limiting myself by only considering relations with men within 30 miles of Los Angeles?

My dad and I last about an hour on the trails and then head to the gym so I can stretch and shower before my noon date with Older Oliver. At the check-in desk, my dad asks the attendant, "Can Match.com members work out here?"

(Awkward nervous laughter from the attendant.)

Apparently my life is a joke. Great.

We stretch, split to shower and then reconvene in the lobby. As we walk to the car he tells me I look beautiful. I roll my eyes. This is date number something out of, well, A LOT this month. It's not a prom.

Dad drops me off at the Getty Center and goes to work at a nearby coffee shop. I walk up the parking lot stairwell and meet Older Oliver at the tram station. He is wearing jeans, a soft pink T-shirt, and a ***cap***. With his hairline covered, he looks younger than before. He looks even more handsome than I recall. I think he is the type of handsome that grows on you.

We have lunch and then find the docent for the architecture tour. She points out that the cream travertine blocks are cut into 30" x 30" squares to give the expansive complex a sense of "human scale." She encourages us to look down at the squares and says, "You will probably each be standing in your own square, unless you are with someone, of course."

I turn my eyes to the ground and note that I am isolated in the center of my own square. Oliver's feet are planted in the adjacent square but touching the boundary between his and mine. I wonder if he is having the same thoughts I am right now. (Yeah, right, he's probably wondering how this loony chick convinced him to sacrifice his Saturday at the Getty.)

I wonder if, even though I say I'm opening myself up to all these men, I'm still keeping myself isolated.

Perhaps many men are standing on the edges of the squares all around me, yet I'm standing coldly, distantly, chastely, wearing a turtleneck, with arms crossed in the center of my own square. I wonder if the architect, Richard Meier, expected his squares to cause such confusion in young women.

My thoughts are interrupted by the vibration of my phone. I have a new text message from Woodlands Will:

"You still MIA or are you back on active duty?"

I feel embarrassed and put my phone back in my purse. I'll text him later to let him know I'm still "socially MIA" because my parents are still in town. Truth!

After the tour, Older Oliver and I explore the West building and then part ways so I can meet back up with my dad. As Dad and I wait to turn out of the parking lot, Oliver pulls up beside us. I had intentionally said goodbye to Oliver at one place and met my dad at another for Oliver's sake. It's only our second date, too soon for him to meet my dad.

I wave at Oliver and he smiles back and says, "Hello, there Rachel's dad!" through the open window of his sparkling new red BMW M3. My dad revs the engine (if the pitiful sound coming from my base model Nissan Sentra can even be called that) and calls out, "I'LL RACE YOU!" Oliver laughs.

MEN!

When I get home, my mother and grandmother want to know how my date went. "Nice," I say.

"Just nice?" my mom asks.

"No, really nice," I say, and then elaborate. "Honestly, Oliver's great. I had a really good time with him, but it wasn't a very thrilling afternoon. I could be 'content' with Oliver long-term. But maybe I'm looking for something more thrilling for the short term?"

My mom says, "Well, Rachel, it's not like you let him take you on a thrilling date. You met him at a coffee shop and then invited him to an art center. YOU are creating low-key dates. Slower pace."

She's right. I can't recall any RAGERS occurring at art museums. Most of the other visitors were in their mid 50s. She is so right. I realize I need to test this theory. For my next date with Older Oliver, I will suggest something more, well, thrilling. I should invite him out to the bars with my friends. See if this shark really swims.

Grandma Rose chimes in: "I really like Oliver! His writing seems a step above the others (she hasn't read ALL of the others', but some)— elegant. It's the difference between a twenty-five-year-old and a thirty-year-old."

Tess has forwarded me "Daily Candy," an LA e-guide to fabulous local events. I immediately subscribe (it's a great resource for potential date venues), then write to her: "I LOVE THIS. Thank you! My mom says I SO owe you a Picture Perfect Peter."

Tess replies immediately: "I like the way your mom thinks."

I log into Match.com. Current totals: 59 "interest" notifications and 87 messages.

I find the following:

- *Email Subject: "I want to get caught in the rain with you."* Kind of corny, but kind of cute that he actually read my profile and picked up on my affinity for getting caught in the rain. I check out his profile and note that he mentions "unisex bathrooms" under the heading "favorite hotspots." Ew. Moving on.

- A message from someone with creepy photos and quite a funny profile. I'd like to comment. Scratch that, I'd REALLY like to quote and comment. But I fear for my life. This guy could be a nutcase. Perhaps even come after me, so I'll keep quiet and not stir up trouble with a perceived LUNATIC. See, I'm not saying there aren't some total WACKOS on Match.com, I'm just saying that there are also some real winners. ☺

- A few follow-up emails from guys who tried me last week and were ignored. My heart breaks.

- A profile that reads: *"I really like to sleep. I also really like women that smell good and can bowl a strike. That's mandatory unless you're like really hot."*

- A man that writes, under "My pets": *"I recently got a pug but have realized I am not ready to be a father so if you want to take a chance on me you could even end up the owner of an adorable pup."*

- A message from a 29-year-old executive manager from a nearby beach town: *Subject: "Congratulations." Message: "YOU HAVE WON the chance to go on a date with ME. This is a once in a lifetime opportunity. You have been selected from MILLIONS. Don't pass up your prize!"*

- A message from a guy who is either a nutcase or has an incredibly wacko sense of humor: *"I have looked at your photos and read every line of your profile. I have already met you, dated you, married you, and divorced you. Thank you for all the memories. Love Hank. Ps. You can keep the country house but I get the RV and our sextuplets."*

- A message from a man who is also new to the *"aria"* (area?). Seriously, whatever happened to putting your best foot forward? I could write a list of Match.com things that irk me. It would include abundant spelling errors in profiles, men who post photographs of their abs, men who don't smile in their photos, and usernames like "SquirrelsNmybutt" (like I said, I couldn't make this up if I wanted to).

- A message from a guy who writes: *"I'm looking for a girl whose picture I want to carry in my pocket because I can't look at her or think of her without smiling. I'm looking for a girl who knows more than me about a lot of things. I'm looking for a girl who loves both dive bars and fine dining, who is passionate and articulate, and who is looking for a guy that wants to explore with someone, laugh with someone, and care for someone. You could be what I'm looking for. Please let me know if I could be what you're looking for."*

My MOM wants to date him. My uncle Fred wants to marry him. He could be the guy for me. But, after reading his profile, I know I'm not the girl for him.

I admit that it is possible that a guy might know better than I that we'd either get along grand or not at all. I've realized that during this journey. So, maybe I too can have the foresight to see that I'm not a certain person's match, even when they might disagree.

In his profile, he mentions that he seeks someone who loves to spend time in lake and ocean waters. I'm afraid of BOTH lake and ocean waters. He wants someone who would not only be excited to play with his canine pal, but who also has her own dog. I don't have a dog and I wouldn't love his dog. I won't even like his dog. The first time the dog licked my face, I might run out the door and jump in to the (SCARY!) ocean water. Seriously. He spends most of his free time going to the movies. I can hardly sit through an entire film. His personality seems fantastic but his interests conflict with mine.

And he's divorced. That, to me, is intimidating. Perhaps because of my age, I'm incredibly hesitant to be open to someone who's been in a (failed) marriage.

I realize it is a bit unfair. Certainly there are things about me that if a prospective boyfriend knew upfront, he might not be interested any longer. Luckily, Match.com doesn't have a line for that in my profile. And, honestly, if I listed all my self-perceived shortcomings, I wouldn't give myself the opportunity to a find a guy who, after falling for me, could potentially cherish my flaws.

This holds true in how I present myself physically in my profile as well. I display photos in which I look my best, but I still want to attract a guy who will love me at my worst.

Go figure.

Earlier today I thought: I'm going on more dates now than I have in the last six months combined. I should probably take the time to tweeze my eyebrows. Even the most down-to-earth guy might be wary of dating a girl with a bridged brow, and I have yet to find a profile that states "actively seeking seniorita unibrow." So I'm not sure what the answer is. Do I post photos of me from my "best angles" and hope that the man I find is just as attracted to the woman I am on the days I'm hormonal, in saggy old sorority sweat pants, wearing no makeup, or worse—super emotional and therefore displaying a face caked with running mascara?

Or do I post the sweats photos and hope for a guy who reads my line about being easily enthused and sees through my tangled nest of a hairdo and unkempt shell to the gem that hides inside?

MY BEST FRIEND FROM CHILDHOOD NOW THINKS I AM A LOOOOOOOOOOOOOOOOOOOOOSER

Today my parents are leaving California. As usual, my dad arrives 40 minutes AFTER the time he and my mom agreed to depart for the airport. He has a few excuses ready. She believed him the first 17 times he did this to her.

Uncle Carl enters the kitchen and tries to lighten the mood by giving my dad a blazer that he doesn't wear anymore. It is bright yellow, so my dad loves it. My mom remarks, "You look like a UTI." (UTI: Urinary Tract Infection. I know, polite.)

My parents begin to argue. They know how to really irk each other. Yet they also know each other's favorite foods and exactly what words the other likes to hear. They have been married for twenty-five years. This is the precedent of love that I witnessed growing up.

If I went on a date with a Match-man and his attire screamed "UTI," I probably wouldn't go out with him again. If he pushed my buttons, I probably wouldn't let him have second date either. How did my parents make it to date 10? How did my mom know that my dad was the one for her, even though he dressed like an unpleasant nether-region infection (she often says "parakeet," but now that I've heard her say UTI, I find it much funnier)? If, on that steamy summer day that they met in a shopping mall, he had been holding a sign that warned "horrifically stubborn and unable to admit when I'm wrong," would she have invited him back to swim in her pool? Probably not. Would I even be here to ponder this? Probably not.

Had she discounted him for his faults, she would have missed finding his charms. That while he's stubborn, he's also delightfully charismatic, wittily insightful, and able to make her laugh heartily. That he had it in him to love her unconditionally and eternally, that she was meant to journey through life with him by her side. She took the time to learn that while there are many things he is not, she cannot live without the things that he is.

From the kitchen, I can see into the dining room where a portrait of Grandma Rose hangs. A few weeks ago, Grandpa Sam told me the story behind it. While serving our country in WW2, he kept a tiny photograph of Grandma Rose in his pocket. In Trinidad in 1945 he paid a local artist one shilling (about 15 American cents) to create a painting from the photograph. He kept the painting with him in the army to remind him of all that he saw as happiness, comfort, beauty, and love.

In 2006, Grandma Rose and Grandpa Sam renewed their vows. In front of all of the guests they tore up the dance floor to their favorite Rat Pack songs. I remember watching in wonder as Grandpa guided Grandma gracefully across the floor. True, they move a bit slower than they did back in the 1940s, and yes, perhaps he has forgotten some of the insignificant conversations they may have had over the years, but he has not forgotten a single step. He has not forgotten how to dance with her. And he never will. There are weeks when it is difficult for him to walk. But I have never seen him struggle to dance with her. He makes it look effortless. With her in his arms, on a dance floor, he is as strong, agile, and graceful as he ever was. Their dance is timeless.

My paternal grandmother, Grandma Anne, has been incredibly blessed, for she has had two great loves in her life. My grandfather Joseph, who passed away in 1996, loved her enough to want her to be happy, with or without him; it was he who encouraged her to seek love again.

She remarried a fellow widower. They are each other's early morning tennis and crossword competitors, travel companions, and duplicate bridge partners. When she had rotator cuff surgery and spilled soup on the floor in a one-armed attempt to ladle out soup for a grandchild, he came immediately to her rescue and cleaned it up, her silver-haired knight in shining armor.

On a vacation in Mexico, she and I walked behind him, and she exclaimed, "Wow, he has GREAT legs."

I still recall how stunning she looked on her second wedding day, in a midnight-blue sequined dress, beaming, surrounded by their friends and cumulative twelve grandchildren. I've attended quite a few weddings by now, but I have to say, my grandmothers have made the most beautiful brides.

On Grandma Anne's wedding day, I was aware of her two loves: the love she affirmed for Grandpa Albert as she vowed to stand by him "in sickness and in health," and the love she had for Grandpa Joseph, which most likely inspired in her an appreciation for love (people with happy marriages who are widowed are very likely to remarry).

These are the standards of love I've been taught. Again, the word Paper-Perfect Peter used comes to mind:

"Momentous."

My conscious returns to the kitchen as my uncle Fred exclaims, "We are COOL DUDES." He is now wearing one of uncle Carl's brightly colored jackets as well.

My mom exclaims, "Chirp chirp sing the Matching parakeets!"

My sister Sophie and I shuffle mom and dad into the car, shuttle them to the airport, and then head to Santa Monica. On the way, we call our dear family friend Bea, so that I can tell her about my recent escapades. Her reaction shocks me.

Bea thinks online dating is superficial and that I should just meet people "in real life."

I give her a recent account of what it's like to MEET SOMEONE in real life. Two weeks ago, at the gym, a guy walked up to me. He stood about 10 inches away from me, stared at me, and said nothing. I waited for him to say, "I recognize you from…" or "I'm a friend of your uncle's," but he didn't. He remained there for about 38 very uncomfortable seconds. On the 39th second I turned to walk away, very creeped out. I headed toward the locker room, fully intending to find my pepper spray in case he approached me again. When I got home, I relayed the events to my uncle, who explained that the boy probably just wanted to meet me, but lost his nerve and froze.

Moral of the story: Real life DOESN'T WORK.

Regardless, she has both POPPED my balloon and RAINED on my parade. She reminds me of my pre-Stella mentality. Of the stigma. I am REENERGIZED and recommitted to my quest. I MUST deliver the truth to the masses. I have become so comfortable with this Match.com thing that I jokingly considered starting a Facebook group titled "Online Dating Is Not Only for Garden Gnome Collecting Spinsters" and listing "Match.com" on my Facebook page under "interests."

On Facebook, I posted a photo I snapped as we drove away from the Getty (the villa on the cliff, under a romantic pink sky, watched by a pale white moon) and Sophie added the caption: "Dashing Getty, are you too on Match.com?" Was I embarrassed? No! There's no shame in online dating!

Bea persists. "Don't you think it's a bit weird and shallow? Looking at someone's photos, income, hobbies, and then deciding if you want to meet?"

I reply, "NO, the convention is shallow."

Think about it:

Guy spots girl at bar.

Girl's top is 78.4% more revealing than those she wears the other six nights a week.

Guy's beer goggles send message to his beer-buzzing brain: JACKPOT. Porn Star body with face of Penelope Cruz.

Pumping with alcoholic confidence, guy moves in for the kill. Yes, I'm intentionally painting this as an animalistic picture. Feel free to visualize male as a lion, female as a graceful gazelle.

Guy gallantly arrives in front of girl and brilliantly and eloquently mutters: "Hey."

Next, either:

Girl is wearing her own dainty beer goggles and believes Hugh Grant has approached. It is too loud for her to have heard his words (WORD), but she doesn't care.

Girl is 110% sober (always multiply actual sobriety by a factor of 1.1 in the context of many drunk people). Girl is aware that said guy is not fully himself and that her shirt is "asking for it." She feels no butterflies in her stomach or serendipitous chemistry. However, there's nothing better on the horizon. She settles, allowing smelly (poignant mix of rum, cigarettes, and sweaty bar air) beast to go in for the kill.

Girl is neither wasted nor sober but is pleasantly chilling someplace in between. Girl rejects boy or, worse, puts him down in front of her friends. Guy's confidence takes a hit. Guy is less likely to make the first move in future situations.

Further, the CONVENTION is based purely on superficialities. Guy approaches girl based on looks because he doesn't KNOW anything else about her. On the Internet, yes you see a photo and learn roughly what the person looks like, but at the very same time, you learn that they are "looking for someone to make chocolate chip pancakes with." Internet dating actually creates the opportunity for me to be initially attracted by someone's confession that they're sick of "their aunt's trying to pimp them out because they can't find a girlfriend on their own" rather than by their biceps.

Bea jabs me again! "But what about serendipity? Don't you think you're limiting yourself?"

I reply, "NO! It's not like I'm wearing those tragic peripheral vision blockers they put on the horses of Central Park! If, en-route a date, I meet my dream dude while pumping gas at the Exxon station, well, that would be great. But I'm not putting my money on it, nor do I want to put all my eggs in one 'chance' basket. I'm taking my destiny into my own hands."

She pushes me further: "If you're looking for a guy that loves art, why can't you just go spend time in the art galleries and meet him there?"

"First of all, I don't have ten hours a day to waste sitting at a gallery counting on the minuscule chance that Mr. Right will happen to be craving a side of Monet AND because then I'd be limiting myself. What if I'm meant to be with someone that doesn't attend gallery events? I went on a date with a PILOT, Bea. I went on a date with a THIRTY-YEAR-OLD. I would not have met these people any place other than Match."

Maybe something in my voice gives away how hurt I am that she disapproves. Her tone takes a step toward apologetic as she says, "I'm just shocked. It isn't like you to fearlessly meet up with strangers you met online."

My tone takes a step toward "I know what you really want to say" as I reply, "I know, Bea, but that's one of the remarkable outcomes from all of this. I am growing. I am changing. Last month I never would have thought I could do this. Our generation has grown up with the Internet. We've seen the 'BEWARE of Internet predators' news specials. We've been conditioned to keep our guard up, to be aware, to be afraid. We've watched enough TV, read enough articles, listened to enough radio programs, to know that anything and everything can give us cancer and the world is a scary, scary, dangerous place. This is not the world that our grandparents grew up in, where people were 'all good at heart' and anyone wearing an army uniform could hitch a ride.

Couple those external messages with the fact that I am naturally a careful, conscientious, "Don't step on the cracks" type of person.

Remember that time I accidentally got left behind at Blockbuster? And as soon as I realized my family had left me, I went straight to the checkout and explained that I was a lost child and directed the cashier to phone my parents immediately? And one of our NEIGHBORS recognized me but I wasn't sure who she was? She told the employee that she could give me a ride home. And do you remember what I did? I raised my voice (per the policeman who visited my elementary school's instructions) and clearly stated, slowly, and with perfect enunciation: "THIS WOMAN IS NOT MY MOTHER and SHE wants me to get INTO HER CAR."

Bea, during my first six months here in California I wasn't meeting many new people because I was fundamentally averse to talking to strangers. And look at me now.

That night, I lay in bed browsing Match.com while watching the Miss America pageant with my eighteen-year-old cousin Josie. Josie says whatever comes to her mind; she has no filter.

"Why are there such cute guys on here? They can't find girls?" she asks.

"I'm cute. I'm on here," I joke.

"Ha, true," she says.

I persist. "But think about it, it's hard to meet people at bars. Besides I don't spend most of my time in bars nor do I want to meet someone who does. I spend most of my time in traffic. I don't meet people in traffic. And I don't think it's healthy to limit the people you could potentially have relationships with to the people you work with."

"Do you think any of these guys are perverts?" Josie asks.

"I used to think Internet sites were for mostly perverts, but not anymore."

"I want to see your profile. I want to see your photos," she says.

I pull up my page and click through the seven photos I have posted.

"Ew, take that one down, you look constipated," she remarks as I conclude the slide show.

"Did you check out your competition?" she asks.

"Before I joined."

"Do you pay for this?"

"Yes, thirty dollars a month."

" I want to join Match.com," she says.

I really need to start a tally of my Match.com converts. I wish there were incentives to get others to sign up. At the gym I recently joined, I will receive a free personal training session if one of my friends joins. Now, if Match.com had a similar program, I'd be rolling in personal training sessions. Pretty soon, I'd be revising my profile to read "Athletic and Toned" rather than "Slender."

I tell Josie, "No, you don't want to join Match.com. You're in college. College IS Match.com- it's a filtered selection of potential boyfriends. It's an artificial environment filled with people with whom you share interests and lifestyle. You don't need Match.com. You're too young for Match.com.

Sunday, January 31

NO KISSING ON THE FIRST DATE, UNLESS THERE IS A SCIENTIFIC REASON TO BELIEVE THAT A PRINCE WILL APPEAR

This morning I'm a half a mile from my house before my alarm sounds. Lately, I've felt as if I have extra energy that needs to be burned off. I'm running so much that the excessive time spent with a wet jog bra rubbing against tender skin is starting to create an open sore on my upper rib cage like the semester I trained for my first half marathon. It hurts. I know I need to tone it down, but I need this time alone along the pavement to clear my head. I start thinking about how people "inflate" their profiles, about how men aren't 100% accurate. Instead, they give themselves an extra inch, or three...

As I return to my driveway, race through the side garden and upstairs to my room, and take a seat at my desk, I consider:

What if, on my profile, I was 100% upfront? What If I listed:

-Sometimes I have a to remind myself to put people before work.

Subtract 15% of respondents

Even now, as I write this, my sister is packing. I want to help her but I'm glued to the screen, writing. I know that spending time with her should be my first priority, yet I don't want to pause my project. This is what I like least about myself. My dedication to literary and architectural creative outlets serves me well, but takes up time that could otherwise be spent with those I love. I call my sister in to read this before even hitting save. I want her to know that I see this as my most glaring flaw. Not just as a potential girlfriend, but as a big sister, a daughter, a friend, a human. Her eyes tell me she knows, but loves me nonetheless. Her eyes tell me the "nonetheless" comes from the many nights I let her sleep in my bed when she was a terrified thumb sucking (ew, drool) 5-year-old, the years I let her ransack my wardrobe while at college, the weekends I returned home and we shared my bed and snuggled just as close as we did when she was so little. Her eyes tell me the "nonetheless" is because I nurture her, I protect her. But to a stranger, there's no "nonetheless." Character flaws that become illuminated in time, if showcased upfront, are DEAL BREAKERS.

-I'm not naturally easygoing, nor do I just "go with the flow" (many men list that as a highly desirable characteristic on their profiles)

Subtract 25% of respondents

-I'm writing a book, and if you message me, three million teenage girls and perhaps just as many middle-aged women may get to read your words.

Subtract 99% of respondents

(And understand that the remaining 1 percent live with their mother, or are also writing a book about Match.com.)

Sophie tells me it's time to go to the airport. As we head for the door, I call out to uncle Carl, "I'm taking Sophie to the airport, meeting someone for coffee, and I'll be home by 4 pm."

"Ha, efficient!" he laughs.

"I have to be!" I reply.

After I drop Sophie at LAX, I call Cocky Connor to let him know that I'm on my way to meet him at Father's Office (a Santa Monica burger place) as planned. He had initially suggested we meet at his apartment and then travel in one car. I politely declined.

In response to my "on the way" heads-up, he answers:

"Great, I just jumped out of the shower, I'll see you there soon!"

When he mentions the word "shower" I instinctively picture him in the shower, then blush. I wonder if he dropped a line that subtly involves nudity on purpose. Hmmm. Okay who's head is in the bathroom here? Mine or his?

We sit at an outdoor table along the street and are both very chatty. Sometimes his eyes wander while I speak, but I'm not sure if it's because he's easily distracted (the streets ARE distracting) or if I'm just boring him.

I apologize, again, for my initial insulting email to him. He assures me, "Really, it's fine."

He explains that he goes on Match every time he moves to a new city (he had two short stints out of LA, one in Chicago and one in Miami), but that he only lasts about three weeks at a time. Apparently, he too gets an overwhelming response. I'm guessing it's because he lists his income ($150,000 +) on his profile. I consider mentioning that, but decide against it. I do, however, let him know that I've set up my Microsoft Mail inbox to automatically send any emails/notifications including the word "Match" to a separate folder so that my inbox doesn't get clogged. This "Match" folder in my normal email inbox now includes 278 emails.

After almost an hour of talking, he suggests we part ways. He has somewhere he's running off to; I wonder if it's to another date. Really.

As we walk to the parking garage, he says, "You're really cute."

When we approach my car, I turn to say goodbye and he gives me a hug. His hand lingers on my lower back.

He leans in to kiss me.

I turn my head.

He calls me out, accusing "I just tried to kiss you and you turned away."

I reply, "I just met you!"

He says, "Okay, okay come here," and gives me little peck on the cheek. "I'd like to see you again."

I smile politely, but don't respond verbally.

A few minutes after I drive out of the garage he sends me a text message:

"Thanks for the date today!"

I reply:

"Sorry, I'm not a first date kiss kind of girl...usually not even a second date kisser either... just attempting to be honest not awkward..."

He writes back:

"No kiss on the second date either??? That honestly might just be a little too conservative for me I think."

I respond:

"Your call. I like to be frank about everything and rather you know sooner than later."

I don't expect to hear back from him.

Judging by his "shower comment" and "kiss attempt," I suppose he may be used to getting "easy cookie." Well, I'm a SMART COOKIE, so getting a kiss from me is no piece of cake!

My phone vibrates as I receive a text from Med-School Mat, who I began corresponding with on Match. He's a 25-year-old med student whose profile reads:

So I signed up for this thing and later embarrassingly told my friend about it. He wanted to know what I wrote for my profile and I refused to tell him. I re-read it later (alone), and laughed at how lame I sounded. Here's a more accurate description of things I like. I'm not sure if you will know me any better for it… In brief: I like to surf a lot. I am a medical student. I love music (taste mostly inline with pitchfork – yeah I know what you're thinking). I have two bicycles; one of them does not have brakes. I wear v-necks and plaid. I play a little guitar. I have a motor scooter. Sometimes, I grow mustaches. I think life is generally funny. I can be serious when I need to be. I have two younger brothers, an older sister and a younger sister. I love coffee and drink a lot of it. Sometimes people I meet don't believe I am going to be a doctor. I usually take that as a compliment. I love the ocean and everything that comes with it. My name is Mathew but I go by Mat. I think these profiles are silly, but I get it. Please say hello.

His text reads:

"So I'm trying to study and looking out my window at what a beautiful day it is. I know it's super late notice but if you're not busy how would you feel about meeting in Venice for coffee and a walk? There's this place in Venice called Intelligentsia that's pretty cool design-wise."

Little does he know that the architect I work for DESIGNED one of the Intelligentsia coffee shops AND that I'm becoming a dog from one of Pavlov's experiments. When I smell tea I automatically assume "date demeanor." That, and, I am turning into a tea bag.

I'm already on the Westside, so I meet him (from the safety of my car) at his Westwood apartment so we can caravan to Venice. He lives just blocks from Tess. I find myself thinking that if he and I don't hit it off, perhaps I'll introduce him to Tess. They could have quite the convenient relationship. Is it bizarre that I'm already thinking ahead of logistics like that?

Deep breath, here goes another "double header" day.

He approaches my car and I step out and introduce myself. I then say, "my best friend in California, Tess, lives around the corner. I know this area very well because I am a morning person- even after a crazy night out at the bars. So when I crash at Tess's I wake up and run until she's up. One time the fact that I run saved my butt. My friends got sick on New Year's and I had to get them home from the club in Hollywood but didn't know the way to Tess's. My uncle picked us up and was able to get within five miles of here by guesswork. Once he got us that close, I was able to recognize the streets from my 'detox' morning hangover runs. So, I was able to figure out how to find my way back to her apartment."

Once I finish the story, I say, "Wow, I don't know why I just told you that. Not what you'd expect someone to blurt out following introductions, right?"

He smiles.

He asks, "Which route do you want to take to Venice?"

I reply, "I'll let you decide since I'm newer to the area AND I'm a horrific driver. Further, if we only find tight parallel spaces I may need you to climb into my car to park it for me."

He says "ok then," smiles again, and gets into his car.

I realize that parking/driving issues are becoming a reoccurring theme. No, I am not proud of this.

Med-School Mat pulls in front of me, I follow.

At the stoplights, I make notes about my date with Cocky Connor and the unsolicited kiss. Med-School Mat watches from his rear view mirror.

He finds a spot for his car and after he parks I motion for him to come get in the driver's seat of mine. I climb into the passenger seat. We find a spot but it's on the other side of the street so we'll need to drive past it to the nearest intersection in order to turn around. There are a line of cars behind us and some approaching ahead. Without thinking I open the door and dart across to stand in the space to "reserve it." I shout, "OK GO TURN AROUND and come back!"

Then I realize I just told a stranger to drive away from me, in my car. Crap.

I yell out "AND DON'T STEAL MY CAR!"

Geez, my life is awkward.

He parallel parks my car perfectly and tosses me the keys.

He strikes me as young, perhaps because he is so tall and lean. It as if he's recently had a growth spurt, and his body is still catching up horizontally to it's new verticality. However, he has the type of face that I can easily imagine aging. That I can picture HOW it will age. I look at his face and effortlessly visualize what it will look like one or two decades from now. He just has one of those faces.

Physically, I don't think he's what I thought I was looking for. Walking alongside him, my eyes are almost level with his armpit. He's so slender that I'm not confident he could carry me. However, he smiles easily and casually, and his smile makes me smile.

Once seated at Intelligentsia, we order a pot of green tea to share. I'm excited to find out that like me, he's a closet tea coinsurer.

"When did you start drinking tea?" he asks.

"Well, when I was a little girl, my dad would take me tea tasting every year at Harney. It was just something special we did together."

As I share this memory, I recall the tasting room's endless rows of wooden shelves lined with tins of tea. My dad and I would choose the two most exotic sounding teas to try. I learned not to hastily eat the crystallized sugar on the counter like rock candy, but to drop it into a steaming cup and watch it dissolve and sweeten the mixture. I learned to patiently wait for the brewing timer to beep before taking the first sip. At some point over the years I understood that these experiences were less about learning the rituals of tea and more about spending time with my dad. Still, when I moved to California I removed three pairs of high heeled shoes from my suitcase so that I could bring three tins of Harney & Sons® loose tea and still comply with the airline's fifty pounds of luggage per passenger limit.

"What about you? When did you start drinking tea?" I ask.

"Well, I smiled when you mentioned sharing tea with your dad because I had a girlfriend who learned a lot about tea from her dad, who was a Taiwanese immigrant. In turn, I learned a lot about tea from her. Then, between undergrad and med school I took a year off to work in a research lab and travel to southwest China, near Vietnam. I was taught how to hold a cup of tea properly, and that it's different for men and women. There were so many customs surrounding tea, it was an incredible way to learn about Chinese culture. But I suppose I can trace my interest in tea back to High School, when I worked in a coffee house. During slow shifts I'd have fun making different drinks. I guess that was when I really began experimenting with tea."

The warm cups in our hands seem to have a calming effect, settling any first date nerves. At a comfortable pause in the conversation, Med-School Mat takes advantage of the opportunity to look around at the coffee shop. His eyes curiously scan the walls, tables, and ceiling. He notices that the ducts hanging above are exposed and comments that he likes spaces where that is the case. A med student with an eye for design? I point out other strategies employed to give the space its atmosphere, and he says, "Wow, I never would have noticed that. See, this is why I love to go places with my friend who is studying architecture. Wherever we go he points out things that I never would have noticed."

"That's why I love to go to new 'scene' bars and restaurants. Most go for the food, or to be seen. I go to look around, for the visual stimulation" I say.

He responds, "I'm a full-time student, so sometimes it's hard to afford those 'scene bars and restaurants'."

"I know! Even going to the ART museums to look around can really add up. I could easily burn through one hundred dollars a week on the entrance fees. I didn't have a job when I first moved to LA so I made a chart of which days each museum offered free admission. I was able to find at least one for each day of the week. I kept it in my glove compartment so that if I ever had an hour to spare, I could drop in for some free art. That's how art should be, anyway. Don't worry, as an 'intern architect' I'm a bit like an apprentice or a med student in rotation. We get lots of work experience but not so much compensation, right? My lifestyle currently is a lot like that of a student. We are totally on the same page as far as that goes."

My own words, "on the same page," brings my book to mind. Hopefully, we'll be on quite a few of the same pages.

We occasionally divert our eyes, when we catch each other smiling simultaneously. Maybe because it's uncomfortable for a stranger to know how much you're enjoying yourself.

After we finish the pot of tea, we walk into the strong sunlight to wander in and out of the shops along Abbot Kinney. I'm talkative because I'm taking pleasure in his company and therefore there are a few times where we both start talking at once. I'm louder, so although my voice trumps audibly, I stop and apologize because I really am sorry. I want to know what he had started to say. Really.

He's soft spoken, but it's not as if he has nothing to say, but rather, he's careful as to how he says it. The word "precise" comes to mind. He could be described as "quiet," but his lack of volume is complimented by a discernibly high air of self-confidence. However, he's not "loudly" confident. He's simply, modestly, quietly, yet powerfully comfortable with himself.

We pass an exceptionally intricate sewer grate, and I blurt out "Wow, that sewer is great!"

I realize what I've just said, and laugh. He didn't catch my pun (great-grate), so I explain. Perhaps grammar jokes are considered dorky, but I don't mind showing him that side of me. His lack of self-consciousness is infectious.

He chuckles, lightly, either because my pun was funny or because he thinks it's funny that I find grammar funny.

I change the subject by asking what enticed him to join Match.com and how long he's been on it.

"I've been on the site about a week. A friend of mine went on it, and she's awesome, and she LOVES it and told me to join. Before I heard her talk about it, I had no idea 'normal' people were on it," he says.

I chime in "That was my case too! It really takes someone you know and respect mentioning they're on Match for you to really believe it's not only for crazies!"

I think about this book. It dawns on me that I can be "that friend" to certain readers. For the first time I am consciously aware that I am the main character in my own book. It is a new type of "self awareness" different than any I have ever experienced before. I need to transcend being merely a character in order for those who read this book to view online dating as a viable option. But, I realize that in order for that to happen, you, the reader, need to get to know me well enough to regard me as a friend. I need to be real to you, so that the fact that I'm on Match.com can inspire you to consider online dating without feeling sketchy or lame. Therefore, in the upcoming chapters I will make a conscious effort to open up, a bit.

I'm brought back to the scorching Venice street as Med-School Mat continues, "besides, 'Med school doesn't leave me a lot of spare time to meet people and it can be a bit incestuous.'"

(I suddenly realize he could be study buddies with Paper-Perfect Pete, my date number one.)

I admit to him, "I can't remember who contacted whom first, do you?"

"Well, when I started I didn't really understand how the site works. I thought 'favoriting' someone was like book-marking them so that you could easily return to their profile at a later date. I didn't realize they'd be notified that you flagged their page. I think I 'favorited' you and then you messaged me."

"OH MY GOODNESS! I thought the same thing and made the same mistake when I first got on the site!" I exclaim.

We both laugh.

"And," he continues, "I'm not usually the type to just approach a girl and make the introduction."

(I could've guessed that about him.)

We've been walking and talking for about three hours, and I start to get antsy to return home to write. I suggest we head back to the cars, but really, I could go on as we are for three more hours.

As we say goodbye, I think about what I would do if HE leaned in to kiss me. I would probably turn my cheek and consider his attempt inappropriate and premature. But I wonder if I would like it? For him to kiss me. Not today, but one day. I think so.

I tell him I'd like to see him again, maybe later this week. He tells me he'd like that.

I get into my car, which he parked generously with extra room in front so that I could easily navigate out. As I speed along the 405 I think about kissing. About how Cocky Connor's kiss shocked me, and my imaginary kiss with Med-School Mat briefly intrigued me. I think about princesses kissing frogs. How many frogs will I have to kiss to find my prince? But, the confusing thing is that there really aren't any frogs here. There are a lot of princes. They're just not all the prince for me. And I don't know how many dates it will take to find the prince for me, or if I'll even know when I find him. If the Cinderella story took place in this era, it would read much differently. Cinderella would have more than one ball each night. She would go from one suitor to the next, without losing any slippers (but maybe a bit of sleep) in between. She would have her pick of princes. She would be Miss Match.com, choosing between Prince Charismatic, Prince Clean Cut, Prince Cuddly, and Prince Charming (among others).

Nowadays Cinderellas have cell phones, GPS, Cosmo, and search engines. So, what's our excuse for being SO lost?

My phone vibrates; I have a text from Prince Med-School Mat:

"It was nice to meet you and a good study break. Let me know if you're free later in the week and want to hang out."

As I approach my exit to the 101, I can see the Getty Center illuminated in the distance, perched on a cliff like a white castle. A tram carrying people up the dark track spills little bits of warm light from its windows. I think of when I last rode that tram. I think of Prince Older Oliver.

STICKS AND STONES
WILL BREAK MY BONES
BUT MATCH WILL NEVER HURT ME?

I wake up early to sit in bed and write. In my lavishly feminine bedroom, the ruffled sheets, pleated duvet cover, embroidered pillows, wicker furniture, oversized lampshades, lace table skirts, and wooden shutters are all white. However, the dreary light from the nearby window dulls the whites to gray. Today is a gray day.

The dreary light fogging my room drags my mood down to one of solemn contemplation.

It's been a few days since I've heard from Adventure Alex. The steady stream of long letters has come to a halt. Maybe I said something wrong. I don't know. I feel vulnerable.

This is an experiment, an adventure, a string of fun and games. But this is also my life, and my heart. I'm not the type to vault my heart away, nor do I wear it on my sleeve. The men I meet have fair aim at it. I don't fall easily, but when I do, I fall hard. Very hard.

If I fall for multiple men, and they all reject me, will I still publish this? I'd like to say yes, but I'm not sure.

I browse the LA weekly online calendar in search of distraction (and potential date events, seeing as I am now in constant need of them). I find an art show with live music Thursday night at the Hammer Museum (and invite Laughing

Lucas, the closet astronomy nerd) and a LA Philharmonic concert at a Methodist Church Wednesday night.

I log into Match.com and discover a message from "Similarities Steve," a 29-year-old lawyer with whom I seem to have A LOT in common.

He writes:

Subject: Good Morning!

I was really excited to find your profile this morning. Like you, I am very passionate about my profession and have found that unfortunately that passion is rare. I too enjoy travel, am a runner, appreciate intelligence, and take as much pleasure from a quiet night in as from a wild night out. I see you're new to town- I'm a transplant as well, although it has been five years now since I moved to LA from the east coast. I'd love to show you around and "stir up some fun." Feel free to call me if you're interested in getting to know me better: 310-924-XXXX. I've learned that it's hard to gauge if there's any potential by talking online.

Steve

Ps. Rand is also one of my favorite authors. I'll leave you with one of her lines: "She knew suddenly that he was not telling her about himself; he was speaking of her."- Ayn Rand, The Fountainhead

I pick up my phone and dial his number. HAVE I FREAKING LOST MY MIND?!

When he picks up I begin, "Hi, it's Rachel, from Match. I read your message and I completely agree with you about talking on the phone and meeting in person being much more effective and authentic ways to get to know someone."

"That was fast! I messaged you less than an hour ago. You don't waste any time, do you?" he asks.

"Nope! My parents were actually just in town visiting and if you'd written earlier I would have suggested the four of us go on a double date and hike Runyon Canyon since I see you like hiking as well."

(Silence. Apparently it's too early for those type of jokes. Oops. Again, I'm getting sloppy.)

"A double date with your parents?" he questions in disbelief.

"Sorry. I was joking. Here's my real proposal: the LA Phil is performing Wednesday night as part of their Neighborhood Concert Series. I'd love to go. Want to join?"

He replies, "I can't say I love classical music unless I'm in that sort of mood, which isn't often, but I've never seen the LA Phil, and I'll try anything once. So I'm up for it."

"Well, I really have no idea what to expect, and we can stay as long or short as we want," I assure him.

"Ok, I'm excited to meet you, but I'm not sure how long I'll want to stay at the concert," he replies.

I'm a bit bummed; I secretly wanted him to be PSYCHED.

Before I have a chance to wallow in the disappointment, a new message (finally) arrives from Adventure Alex.

RE: and you thought the 1st was long...

To put your mind at ease, you have said many things, and most of them sage, but none of them wrong :).

I'm actually in transit... in Amsterdam at the moment. I should get back to LA about noon on Tuesday. Can I give you a call when I get back in town?

Talk soon!

Alex

I respond immediately:

My week is pretty full but Friday is open... perhaps we can meet then.

Talk soon.

Safe Travels,

Rachel

A DAY WITHOUT A DATE IS LIKE THE 101 WITHOUT TRAFFIC: R A R E AND THEREFORE CHERISHED

Kiesha's "Boots and Boys" blasts from my ipod during my morning run. I picture my closet. Yep, still have more shoes than boys. Phew.

I make a turn for the gym, deciding to "run by" (literally) to lift a few (very light) weights. There is a motorcycle parked by the glass entrance doors and I feel that eerie déjà vu sensation.

I try to place the motorcycle, where have I seen it before? I realize it looks like the one I saw in a Match profile picture. Is that exact Match-man is here, in this gym, working out? It wouldn't be completely impossible, and might even be probable, considering I was searching through profiles exclusively within or near my zip-code.

I think of the other places that I frequent that other Match.com members visit as well. With every Match-seed I plant, am I'm also placing a landmine? At the end of this adventure, will I be left with 2,938,215 places in Los Angeles that are off limits, or that I am afraid to go to, for fear of crossing paths with a "failed Match"?

I make a beeline for the assisted pull-up machine and climb onto its platform. From this lofty position, I can see almost everyone at the gym. There are lots of men. None of them look familiar. Are any of them on Match.com? Have any of them seen my profile but for some reason chose not to message me? Although I'm peering out over a sea of what I consider utter strangers, somewhere, on one of these machines, is there man that recognizes me?

Weird.

If someone here does recognize me, they probably won't approach me, judging from the ocean of sweat beginning to pool on the rubber floor just below me.

I walk over to the rows of personal trainer desks to see about scheduling my "fitness assessment." I meet with a trainer who is "glad to meet me, excited to have a session together, and see if we have chemistry."

I'm a bit irked. I'm looking for chemistry on my dates, now I need to be looking for chemistry in a personal trainer as well? I want to tell him that it's unlikely that we'll have chemistry even if we seem truly compatible (for a trainer/trainee relationship) on paper. I want to tell him that even in seemly ideal conditions, chemistry is rare. I want to tell him that I know this because I am writing a book about it.

I keep my mouth shut.

After we set up an appointment for tomorrow morning, I run home to shower. As I get out of the shower, the digital clock on my bedside table reads 11:56 am.

I remember Adventure Alex returns to the states today and is supposed to call.

Later, on my way home from tutoring, I hit major traffic along the 101 freeway. In Los Angeles, "major" traffic means zero movement. In fact, sometimes you actually roll backwards.

I am saved by classical KUSE. I turn the radio up and unwind to the glory of the LA Philharmonic playing Pomp and Circumstance. I stop chewing on my lip and reach for the carrot sticks I packed in my tote bag. I find it thrilling that today the LA Phil is playing on my car stereo but tomorrow I will be hearing them live.

The tune of the traditional graduation march leads my thoughts to my graduation from college, to my graduation from high school, to the night I heard the St. Petersburg Philharmonic in Switzerland… and then… to Alex.

I'm thinking of him partly because I mentioned hearing the St. Petersburg Philharmonic perform in Switzerland to him in one of my letters, but also partly because something tells me he would be eager to have an opportunity to hear the LA Phil live.

And then something clicks. I grasp the real reason why I wrote him that second email. The one where I "changed my mind" and decided, "maybe he isn't what I'm looking for." Yes, part of it WAS because he reminded me of my first love, and therefore I didn't want to make the same mistake again by choosing the same type of person. That was true.

But, what also prompted me to renege my initial message to him was a sudden feeling of panic. Because I sensed he had similarities to my previous boyfriend, I consequently also sensed that there was a chance I could like him as much as I liked that boyfriend. That there was the possibility that I could not just like, but eventually love him. That I could become as attached and therefore as vulnerable again.

And that was terrifying.

When I wrote the first letter to Alex I was inspired by the potential to know, once again, the level of love I once felt. When I wrote the second letter, it was out of a subconscious fear of the potential amount of pain that the loss of such a love could cause.

I've always said that I don't regret having loved and lost. That, if given the chance, I would live it the same way again. Well, now maybe life is giving me a chance to prove it. If the opportunity to love, to truly and unguardedly love, presented itself, would I take it? Even if loving meant likely losing, would I take the leap?

I want to meet Alex right now.

But too:

I'm afraid to meet him.

I want desperately to be as happy as I once was, but I'm equally petrified of being as hurt.

I think of the time my first love, Charlie, initially told me he loved me. It was winter and we were in southwestern Virginia. A floodlight in the apartment complex's parking lot cast a bluish glow on the windowsill of my bedroom. The air was sharply cold, but the sheets we warm. I snuggled close to him, basking in his body's heat.

Laying on his back, speaking towards the ceiling, he said "I have something to tell you."

He rolled over to his side so that he was facing me, and said, "I love you."

"I love you too," I replied, and wondered if he could see me smiling through the darkness.

"I've been wanting to say it for a long time," he said.

"Me too," I whispered.

Then I remember another night, much later, a night in the midst of our breakup.

I remember sitting awkwardly next to him on my bed. I remember wanting him to comfort me, to hold me. I remember him standing up off the bed, and then laying down on the carpet. I remember laying down beside him, with my head in the nook between his arm and shoulder. I remember that being my most secure place to rest. I remember him telling me he wouldn't let anyone else lay in that precise spot, exactly as I was now, ever. I remember him telling me that he'd always be here for me, that I could call him, and hideaway in the alcove of his frame. I remember knowing that I wouldn't. That I couldn't.

That I couldn't find my niche in the cave of his arms anymore.

I remember feeling wounded, and frightened.

I remember noticing my sinking birthday balloons in the corner of my room. I remember them no longer reminding me of a night of over the top sorority celebration. I remember only thinking that it was time to throw them away.

I remember thinking that it was time to throw a lot away.

I remember comprehending that the one person I had grown dependent on to support me, couldn't support me through this.

I remember we turned the mutual hurt into anger. I don't remember how.

Maybe we did that intentionally. In some ways, anger is easier to bear than hurt.

Charlie stopped talking to me, and I was enraged. It wasn't until about a year later, that I could see that his silence was his greatest parting gift. It forced me to let him and what we had go, completely. It forced me to rebuild my life entirely apart from him.

At this point it has been just over four years since Charlie and I broke up. We have both dated other people. He now lives in an industrial loft in Boston with his girlfriend, Kristin, whom I've met. She is intelligent and poised. He has told me about how they skateboard around their loft after work. That she works as a docent at a museum, and he at an architect's office.

And, I'm okay with hearing about it. What's more, I want to hear about it. I think that's proof that I loved him and on some level always will.

It's a different kind of love. The kind of love where you know you aren't the one to make the other person happy, but you still want them to be happy, and hope that they find that someone that can make them happy.

It took me years to get there.

I realize, after we broke up, what I really missed wasn't only him. It was me. I missed the me I was when I was with him. When I was in love, really in love... everything in my life seemed more saturated, more vivid. I'm not looking to find another him, I'm looking to find me, or the me I was when I was living in love.

Eventually, the traffic starts to flow. I hold my breath as I approach the elevated patch of freeway where the valley glitters like million rows of late summer celadon, pay yellow, and sunset orange citronella candles below.

Wednesday, February 3

THE THINGS WE DO
AND DO NOT WANT
TO HAVE IN COMMON

I hop out of bed, and into my gym clothes. While stretching, I realize that Adventure Alex never called yesterday.

A few days ago, I started to wonder how this book will end. I can't go on like this forever (back to back dates and hours spent writing about them).

One of two things will happen: either nothing will happen or SOMETHING will happen.

Will this drag on endlessly? Or, am I about to encounter a spectacular final chapter to this Match journey?

I don't know. Your guess is as good as mine.

It's past lunchtime. I'm not hungry.

A Match-message arrives from a recent dental school graduate. I respond:

Ok so I realize you're going to think I'm insane, but I think dating a dentist would freak me out. Getting my teeth cleaned is the bane of my existence. I cringe at the thought of gloved hands in people's mouths and that sound of a drill on teeth [eeek, I'm squirming already]. Anything dental-related just really gives me the heeebey-jeeebies!

sorry...

Rachel

He replies:

Rachel,

I knew I should have been an optometrist!

Jared

I shut down my laptop and get in my car to head to the gym for my "fitness assessment." According to the trainer, I have fantastically strong quads and calves, but the backs of my thighs aren't up to par (typical "runner's legs"). He wants to know, on a scale from one to ten, how motivated I am to build up the backside of my thighs? Well, since about one hundred men on Match.com don't seem to be bothered by this particular "shortcoming," I would say my motivation hovers just above 0.0032.

After the gym, I drive to the Wilshire Methodist Church for my LA Philharmonic Concert date. En-route, I text Older Oliver and invite him to Tess's wine tasting birthday party on Saturday. I'm taking my mother's advice by changing up the atmosphere from our previous dates. Oliver responds confessing he already has plans with friends for Saturday. Serves me right for waiting until Wednesday to extend the invitation. Arg.

I meet Similarities Steve in the parking lot. He definitely fits the bill of tall, dark, and handsome... but right off the bat I have an inkling that maybe he's not my "type." But I'm not SURE and I'm tired of being UNSURE. He has a nice smile, but he doesn't smile easily. Or, what I mean is that his face doesn't naturally "rest" in a smile. There is something guarded, and solemn about his face. Maybe he's just had a long, hard day at the office?

On the way to the church entrance, he asks, "Where did you go to college?"

"Virginia Tech" I say.

"Were you a student when...when there was that massacre on campus?"

"Yes" I answer, quietly.

"I was in a similar situation" he explains, and goes on to divulge that he was part of a community that suffered a shooting as well.

I don't want to have this in common with someone.

I don't want anyone to have this in common with anyone.

We enter the sanctuary and I motion towards an empty row and exclaim "Look, edge seats!" He proceeds to enter that row and continues all the way to the far side. He misunderstood my intention. I wanted to have the center aisle seat, so I could actually see the musicians, not sit on the outer edge so that we could prematurely sneak out unnoticed.

The concert begins and the sound overwhelms me. The triumphant music in the context of the vaulted ceiling, the boldly colored stained-glass windows, the rows of pews ahead and in the balcony above, and the conductor dancing about with his back to us, at the front of the room, with the reflections of the six ceiling-mounted double-tier chandeliers glistening in his black patent leather shoes- is too beautiful.

This music, in this context, creates the type of moment in which one yearns for someone to share it with.

In my periphery, I can tell that Similarities Steve is unmoved.

I am abruptly very aware of my tasseled clutch placed against my left hip, between us. This experience is not affecting him, he is apart from it. In my eyes, in this context, he has become an outsider. Further, him watching me feels like a stranger is witnessing me partake in a deeply personal ritual. It feels wrong and uncomfortable. Because he does not value the music, I do not want to share it with him.

The orchestra begins to play Mozart's Overture to The Marriage of Figaro, and I wish my dad were here enjoying this concert with me.

At the conclusion of this piece, muffled by the avalanche of applause, I surprise myself by being the first one to ask, "Ready to leave?" He nods, and we briskly walk out.

I can't recall where we parked; I blindly follow him through the lot. I find my car and he finds his. We hastily bid farewell, without discussion of further dates.

This was my shortest date yet.

I slam my car door shut. I don't exactly know what just happened. Why did this date go so wrong? What I DO know, is that he's NOT the one for me.

I'm "SURE" of it. Fish fish I got my wish.

Am I happy now?

No.

WILL YOU BE MY FRIEND?

I have to be at Lucille's for computer tutoring by 9:30 am and my gas tank is literally on empty. Since joining Match.com, I have been driving asterisks around LA to commute from one date to the next. Therefore, I have gone through gas almost as (if not MORE) quickly than I have gone through men.

Woodland-Creatures Will texts me about getting dinner this Saturday. I want to join him, but only see this progressing as friendship, and don't want to mislead him. I craft him an email to lay it all out clearly:

Hello there!

Re: Dinner Saturday...

Well, the decision's compounded by two issues:

1. I really [as in VERY VERY MUCH] enjoyed meeting you but don't know if we have "chemistry." Regardless, I'd like to see you again, because I'm "on the market" for a quality guy friend "in the neighborhood." BUT, I realize that you, unlike me, are NOT a newbie in LA and so perhaps you are not open to simply making new friends. There were times in college when I felt I had "too many" friends. The saying goes "quality over quantity." I believe a footnote should be added that explains, "further, quantity can seem overwhelming and actually inhibit your ability to be attentive to those few that are truly your quality friends. So, If you choose to tell me to "hit the road Jackie," I'll understand.

2. Saturday is my friend Tess's birthday. As her BEST friend, I am obligated to get drunk with her, in the daylight (she has explicitly told me so- I offered to DD- but she refused, vehemently). The party is from 2-6pm... so I could have dinner with you, but MAY need a ride to the restaurant (chances are I will be ALMOST sober by 6... but NO promises... and, even if there is 0.003% of ONE glass of wine still left in me, I'd STILL rather be safe than sorry). Alas, however, if you're still up for dinner perhaps carpooling wouldn't be such an ordeal if you were thinking something valley-esque, seeing as I can practically SEE your yard from mine (or, well, I probably would be able to if they're weren't any trees/houses).

Cheers,

Rachel

His response astounds me.

Haha... It's all good. I actually knew the chemistry was no good in the first 3 seconds of meeting you. It was funny because when I was mentioning dinner, I wasn't even thinking "date." I was just thinking of doing something fun with someone local, like try some silly or odd place we've never been. I'm going to be looking at condos in the afternoon, so I'll call you when I'm done. If you feel up to it after the party, I can pick you up (feel free to invite your friend too), otherwise, no worries.

~Will

I am incredibly impressed and delighted. No pressure, no stress, just good clean fun right in my own backyard. Thank you Match.com.

I scurry about my room to throw a purse together, grab a granola bar from the pantry, and get into my car to drive to the Hammer Museum to meet Laughing Lucas for our second date.

Wilshire is a stand still. Lucas and I play I-spy from our cars until I miss a light that he makes, and we are separated.

When I arrive in the courtyard café I dial his cell to see where he is.

"I'm right here," he says.

"I don't see you" I reply.

"I'm right behind you," he says.

"No, you're not" I tease (though I can hear his voice a few feet behind me), and I continue to weave about the potted courtyard trees just for kicks before twirling around to greet him.

We walk over to the café window to order sliders and tomato/mozzarella salad and then select a table near the instrumentalists. I position my chair away from the table a bit, as close as possible to the nearest heat lamp. There are candles on the tables, and an illuminated cocktail bar in the center of the courtyard. Museum visitors between various gallery rooms stop to listen to the music on the mezzanine level above, as well as from the tables scattered around us. Children dance in front of the performers, and I watch a young girl drag her father over to spin her around and lift her into his arms. I smile, it reminds me of the outdoor summer concerts from my childhood in Virginia, and of my dad. I wonder if Lucas has intercepted my smile, followed it to the father and daughter pair, and misinterpreted my sentiment. I wonder if he know how far off all of that (settling down, having children) seems to me.

In an attempt to squash any family-building thoughts he MAY possibly be having, I ask him about the script-writing project he mentioned on our first date.

"It's really difficult. I have gotten used to only doing what I love: acting, acting coaching, voice-overs... I've had to realize that just because script-writing is difficult doesn't mean it's not work that I want to do, or work that in some ways I love to do."

I reply, "I know what you mean. I'm incredibly uncomfortable when I'm working on a design puzzle. But, not toiling, not exerting effort to find the solution, is not an option. Just because it's challenging and difficult and uncomfortable, doesn't mean I don't love it or that I could NOT do it. I have to do it. I mean when I first came to LA, before I had a paid job, I was working on an uncompensated design gig. It was time-consuming and demanding. But I still loved the work, which is why I took the project on- without pay. That's the story of my first LA design project: the green show-case house."

He asks, "How did you find that opportunity? How did you get involved in the project?"

"I went to a lecture at the Pacific Design Center and the sponsor of the project was one of the lecturers. At the end of her presentation she announced, to the room of interior designers and architects, that she would like to collaborate with a design team to furnish the show house, but that the design services would have to be provided pro-bono in exchange for the potential media exposure. That night, I formed a design partnership with two of my colleagues from design school. I've always known they were very talented and the plan all along was to open our own firm eventually, but obviously not this soon! The opportunity sort of fell in my lap and I seized it. I had business cards ordered overnight, met with the project sponsor the next morning, and the rest is history. It's been a great ride; the project has opened a lot of doors, including the opportunity to design two original patterns for an organic fabric company. All of the projects we've worked on since have been both creatively challenging and very enjoyable. I don't believe that 'difficult' and 'enjoyable' are exclusive adjectives that can't be used together."

"I completely agree," he replies.

There are long stretches of time where we don't converse. It's not awkward, because we both know we could easily fill the silent spaces and then some. It's also not awkward because the spaces aren't silent. The courtyard is jumping from the jazz, and we share a mutual appreciation for the music. At the end of each song, Laughing Lucas claps loudly. When the lead singer makes a funny noise or catcall, Lucas hoots and chuckles, TOO loudly. But, he always laughs without hesitation, and I like that.

After awhile he asks me, "the museum closes in an hour, do you want to stay and listen or see the exhibit?

"Both," I say. He grins.

We listen a bit longer, and then head for the exhibits.

"It's so cool to be here at night. I love to go to 'daytime' venues at night. It makes me feel sneaky, like I'm not supposed to be here. I have the same feeling when I prance around the LACMA after dark," I say.

"You prance?" He asks, as we walk through a long corridor. "I want to see it. Why don't you prance to the exhibit?"

I politely decline the suggestion.

He strikes me as a caricature of a person: loud, highly animated, immensely entertaining, and full of voices (not all of which seem his own, sometimes he adopts the voice of what sounds like a BIG HAIRY CARTOON MONSTER, for example).

We explore the museum and then the design store for over four hours. He walks me to my car and in parting I say, "Saturday is my friend's birthday and we are celebrating by going wine tasting. I know you don't drink, but if you're interested, I'd love for you to join us. I think you would find it all quite amusing."

I figure even if he comes and doesn't enjoy himself, he's an actor so he can fake it. No, not really. Really, I think he would get along and have a good time with my friends. I want to test that theory. And I don't want to wait a long time before I get to see him again.

He's already double-booked for Saturday, but suggests maybe we could get together on Sunday. Geez... so many guys and a girl still can't get a date?!

"I had another great time. You're really fun," Lucas says.

"Yes, I know," I say.

"What?" he says, "You know you're fun?"

I jump back in "Oh! No, sorry, I mean I AM fun, but what I MEANT was YES we had another great time again, and I think you're fun! I think WE are fun. I was agreeing with you... in that way."

I almost follow that with "I've been on lots of dates with other men since I last saw you and I want to write a book about it." But, I catch myself. Although, for some reason, I really want him to know. I don't want to keep secrets from him.

Friday, February 5

I'm 100% SURE
THAT I LIKE YOU AT LEAST 70%

My general email [NON-MATCH] inbox contains two very important messages:

The first is from the director of the international architecture firm that interviewed me before my date with Paper-Perfect Peter. She's offering me a very modest stipend if I accept the internship at their downtown LA office. If I take the job and start working ten-hour workdays (with a one and a half hour commute), I may have to put Match.com on hold.

Perhaps this is a sign that it's time to return to reality.

The second email of importance is from Tess. It is a one-liner:

"I miss you."

I realize that I have been focused solely on this venture, this book, and have not been keeping up with her. I've become WORSE than one of those girls who are attentive friends until they get boyfriends, and then ditch their girlfriends. I don't even HAVE a boyfriend and I've neglected her this week. But, in my defense, juggling ten potential boyfriends is more time consuming than having one steady one.

I make a mental note to call her after my lunch date with Med-School Mat.

Med-School Mat is busy studying for an exam this week, so we plan to just meet for a quick lunch. I'm wearing my Nikes, gray yoga pants, t-shirt, and old sorority sweatshirt. I hope I look sporty-cute, not sloppy-grunge…

He arrives before I do, waits for me just inside, and opens the door as I approach. It's pleasant to see him again.

I ask him how his study sessions are going.

He replies, "It's tough. But, one of the nice things about med school is that they endorse the idea that one can't know absolutely everything about medicine. Therefore they give us great tools to access information so that when we don't know something, we can research it effectively. It's quite a challenge to go from college exams where I could walk out knowing that I KNEW every answer, to med school exams, where I know that I'll be able to retain 70% of the material, at best. It's a matter of determining which information is the most important. It's tricky."

"So when doctors leave a patient and return, they might be looking something up?" I ask

"Yep" he says.

Geez. I wish that was acceptable in other fields. It would be nice to say to a client, "well, hold on, I'll be back in five," and go wikipedia their specific questions and return an expert.

Or, if Med-School Mat and I are still seeing each other, six months from now, and he says "I love you," and I'm not 100% sure how to respond, would it be acceptable for me to say, "I'll be back in ten minutes, please wait here" and then go review my notes (the pages of this book)?

Does this apply in other ways to relationships? Is there a 70% rule? If you meet someone, and are certain you like him/her at least 70%, does that mean you go on dates until you determine it's closer to 100%? Or until you decide you were wrong, and it's more like 3%?

I've dated guys I liked "just 70%" before, but at the time it made sense. I was lukewarm about Brian. He was attractive, athletic, could hold a decent conversation- he was a catch. But I knew from the moment we began dating that he wasn't "my catch." He was someone else's. So why did I knowingly choose to enter a relationship with someone I felt 70% affection for? The "medical" term would be "rebound." However, that word has negative connotations, which I disagree with.

My breakup with Brian was unemotional and boring because it followed shortly after a more severe breakup (Charlie). With Brian, there was no drama, just mutual parting. Prior to meeting each other, we had both just come out of life changing relationships. We mutually sought a warm body to keep us company at night, to trick ourselves into feeling not so abandoned, until the pain subsided. It wasn't one-sided abuse on my part, it was reciprocal understanding. We were temporarily filling a void for each other, a void that felt like a big gaping hole. We were aware of this, but didn't speak of it. After we broke up we didn't really remain friends because we didn't even have "friendship chemistry." However, I remain grateful for his embrace. I remain grateful for the nights I spent in his arms, imagining he was the man who had recently broken my heart, imagining things were as they had been in months past, when my heart was more than whole- when it was inflated beyond what I had ever considered possible.

While dating Charlie, I felt delightfully hot. So hot, in fact, that the fresh parting burns were intolerable, and, took almost unbearably long to heal. When we broke up, I felt miserably cold. Brian helped me to feel a little bit of warmth, even if it was artificial. I'd like to say our "use" of each other was subconscious, but I sincerely believe we both knew what we were doing. We were just two frozen people, praying that although we ignited no fire in each other, that if we held each other close, we might be able to re-learn how to muster a little bit of warmth.

We helped each other to begin the process of thawing.

It's been years now, and my life is in many ways filled with contentment and warmth.

Currently, I'm not looking for a bed of charmingly glowing embers to kneel by in attempt to assuage nightly shivers or shudders. I'm looking for rapture.

I'm looking fireworks.

I would say at this point, Med-School Mat, Laughing Lucas, and Older Oliver are all men I like "at least 70%." This causes quite the conundrum. The plan was to go on as many dates as it took to find the guy where I meet him and "just knew"- and then I'd stop. However, thanks to the 70% syndrome, I'm not 100% sure. So I'm going on multiple dates, and therefore, I fear, slowly building relationships with multiple men.

Perhaps this voyage has veered off-course. But I don't see an alternative. Because, I don't want to be 70% happy, when I could be 100% enchanted.

I try to focus on the date at hand. Med-School Mat and I finish our sandwiches and he walks me to my car. I insist he let me drive him to his because it's chilly and rainy.

I slide the passenger seat back to accommodate his extraordinarily long legs. The brochures and maps from the Hammer Museum (from my date with Laughing Lucas) lay in a pile at Med-School Mat's feet.

"I've lived on the west side for almost two years now, and I haven't been to the Hammer yet," he says.

"They have lunch time lectures there," I say.

He replies, "That would be fun. Tonight is one of the 'First Friday' events at the Natural History Museum."

"What are 'First Fridays?" I ask.

"It's when they have Friday evening events, concerts, or lectures at the museum," he says.

"Wow that sounds awesome, we should do that sometime," I say.

He replies "Yea, definitely, and we should try one of the Hammer lunch lectures too."

He gives me a hug and after we draw apart we sit still, looking at each other in silence for a moment.

It's an awkward silence, but not to him, only for me. It's awkward for me because I'm uncomfortable with the words with which I'd like to fill it.

I want to tell him everything. That I like him. That I like him at least 70%. That I'm still meeting other people. That I might like them too. That my life has turned into a story, and that I want to share it. And that he is part of it.

I don't fill the silence with any of those words.

Mat steps out of my car and I turn onto Ventura as my phone rings.

Finally, it's Adventure Alex calling. I pull over because with my car-(un)luck, I'm likely to hit a pole if I attempt to chat and drive. We set up a coffee date for later today.

The torrential rain provides a clouded curtain of privacy. Before starting up my car again, I call Tess.

"Hello stranger," I say.

"Rachel!" she is excited to hear from me, especially in the middle of a long workday.

"I'm sorry I've been MIA, life's been crazy. It's another double-header date-day: one down, two to go."

She laughs and remarks, "Your life is awesome."

"Tess, I need your advice. I'm not sure when to tell the Match-men about my book or how to prove to them that the intention to find someone came before the inspiration to write."

"If you tell them too soon, you might spook them. How about on date four? The guy that's right for you, he'll understand, because he'll understand you. He'll get it that you get excited about things and have to explore them with your creativity, in this case with a book. Besides, if he's gotten to know you well enough he'll know your intentions are good. If you tell him too soon, he won't have gotten a chance to know that you're not the type of person capable of 'faking a relationship' to write a book," she concludes.

"I just feel conflicted about what's right, and even about my own feelings. At this point, there are three men that I could end up really, really falling for…and after my date tonight, the total could rise to four."

Tess replies, "You know what I'm going to say. I want you to be happy. You shouldn't quit looking until you find someone that makes you happy and excited. You're living every girl's fantasy. You're going on date after date with eligible bachelor after eligible bachelor!"

I reply, "You're right. It's just all happening so fast. Listen, I have to get back on the road so I make my next date. With the rain who knows how horrible the traffic will be."

"Ha, I bet you do have to get to your next date. Tough life, Rachel!" Tess teases.

"Tess, thank you. For listening and understanding. I hope you know that I AM going to MAKE you get on Match.com."

"Ha ha ha, okay okay…" she laughs.

I hang up the phone; turn off my hazards, and head to the coffee shop to meet Alex. The Starbucks we agreed on is in an outdoor shopping center that has a carousel in the center. While I wait for him to arrive, I look out the window at the ornately painted horses, sculpted golden poles, and blinking brightly colored lights. The bucketing rain blurs the richly detailed, storybook scene into an amorphous haze of glittering light and glistening shapes. Squinting through the band of panes, I eventually discern a dark shape briskly moving from the parking garage, through the carousel plaza, and towards the coffee shop entrance.

A handsome man in a dark coat and tie opens the door, brushes the water from his shoulders, scans the room, spots me, and approaches.

In an unhurried, confident voice, he says, "I'm Alex."

Of all the men I've met so far, he is the closest to what I picture when I close my eyes and imagine my ideal boyfriend. I know that sounds weird, but I believe every girl has one. Think about it. Between relationships, when you're lonely, and reading in your bed, and you picture a man sitting beside you with his arm around you- what does he look like? Mine looks like Alex.

My senses are heightened. I feel as though this is a scene from an old, classic romance movie.

Alex's short hair is sopping wet, and appears darker than mine. I bet it's more of a graham cracker color when dry. Drips of water slide down his face and mat his thick, dark eyelashes. With one strong, quick motion of his arm, he wipes the pooled rain from his lashes and mopped hair. He reaches for a nearby stack of napkins and dries his hand.

He's dapper in both his physical appearance and his demeanor. He takes off his jacket, and I find the fact that he's dressed professionally in a shirt and tie to be incredibly attractive.

This is the first date in which I sense a bit of internal pressure. I want to impress him. But what's more, I want to be infatuated with him. Judging from his letters, I think perhaps he could be what I'm looking for. I want this coffee date to confirm it.

We begin by talking about our jobs. Not because we're straining for conversation topics, but because we're mutually passionate about our careers. We therefore talk quickly and with enthusiasm. I marvel at how articulately he speaks, with outstanding vocabulary and refreshing bits of witty humor.

After listening to him for a few minutes, I am certain that he's brilliant. In fact, I am very aware that he is most likely smarter than I am. This both intimidates me and turns me on.

Looking across the table at this stranger with whom I've already shared so many (written) words, I ask, "What convinced you to join Match.com?"

He explains, "It's actually a cool story. One night I went to In-and-Out-Burger on my way home from work. The drive-through line was pretty long, so I parked and went inside. After I ordered my meal, I sat down at a booth to wait. There was an elderly man in the booth across from me. After a few minutes, an elderly lady joined him. I could tell by the way they greeted each other that they had never met before. I listened as the conversation unfolded, and learned that they had connected online. They had both already had marriages and families. They just wanted companionship and company. It was so amazing. When my dinner was ready and I was about to leave, I really wanted to tell them that they had inspired me. I wanted to tell them that I was going to go home and check out Internet dating sites."

I've asked that same question many times, on many dates. Adventure Alex's answer is the most memorable.

He sat in traffic for two hours to have coffee with me. On our way out, he held the door open for me, and, when we walked towards the escalator he paused to make sure I stepped onto it first. He waited with me at the valet for my car. When my car arrived, I waited for him to say goodbye. I wanted to see if he would mention seeing me again. He did. I was thrilled.

I think I'd like to tell him about my book on the second date. I think he might find it amusing. Or maybe I'd never hear from him again.

When I get home, my aunt greets me. I tell her that I've had two dates today.

"Well, are you in love?" She asks.

I pause. I'm "in confusion." My heart is starting to feel like a scalloped potato, split and frayed in different directions. I shake my head "No."

"Are you wet, cold, and hungry, but feel warm and fuzzy inside?" she asks.

I shake my head "no" again, but just to feeling "warm and fuzzy inside."

I do feel wet and cold.

A GRAND CONNECTION

An alert from my phone startles me awake. I find a text from Laughing Lucas:

"Hey Lady! Change of plans, I'm free starting at two. Am I still invited to Tess's birthday?!"

I call him and he bellows, in a perfect German accent, "GUTEN TAG!"

"Listen, I have to be at the party by 2 pm so I'll ride with Tess. This way you'll also have your car there in case the wine-er-ific-ness starts to wear on you."

"Ok, so if I get sick of you, I can leave. Got it!" he teases sarcastically.

"Exactly!" I laugh.

At 12:45 pm Tess calls. I answer my phone, standing naked in the center of my room, with wet hair. She lets me know she's ten minutes away from my house. The plan was for her to pick me up at 1:30 pm. She's running VERY early.

I have no idea what I'm going to wear. I've been going through a lot of outfits lately. I proceed to put on, and then rip off seven shirts. I hastily dry my hair, stuff a stick of mascara in my purse, and run out the door and into her car (a full twelve minutes after she arrives).

In the car, she asks me how things are going with Lucas. I tell her that I think I should spill all my beans to him today after the party.

"Are you insane?" she asks.

"Maybe," I reply.

"Are you falling for him?" she asks.

"Maybe," I reply.

"Do you want to scare him off before there's a chance?" she asks.

"No" I say.

"It's settled then, no spilling until date four."

"Fine," I concede, and then change the subject to her birthday party.

The wine tasting venue is a hidden nook in Malibu Canyon. Within the entrance gate there is a fire pit surrounded by enough chairs to seat all eighteen birthday party attendees. When Lucas arrives, I motion for him to come fill the chair beside me. Because he doesn't drink, I start by getting us each a bottle of water. Although I leave him surrounded by strangers, he seems at ease. In some ways this is a test. Lucas the actor is "auditioning" for the role of "Rachel's boyfriend."

As I sip my first of several glasses of wine, I unwind. When it starts to drizzle, he offers me his jacket. I politely decline; I'm warm from the wine. He leans over and uses a menu to cover my wine glass so it won't fill with rainwater. At times, I leave him to walk to the bar for another glass. Each time I return, I find him happily talking with the people around him.

Tess's party turns from a daytime to evening event. The other groups of people around us, the entrance, and the hills in the distance fade into darkness. Our eyes are effervescent with the reflections from the dancing flames. Without the starkness and clarity afforded by daylight and bright California sunshine, the party seems more intimate. I scoot my chair closer to Lucas and rest my feet on the slate ledge of the fire pit. I'm not sure who or what is casting a spell over me; Lucas, the captivating flames, or the aromatic wine. Tess is a few celebratory toasts past tipsy. She struts from guest to guest, chatting gaily. I am aware of Lucas watching me happily watching her.

Somehow we end up discussing a book he read about a man who worked in the twin towers the year of the terrorist attacks. The man wasn't in his office when the planes hit because he was having an affair at a nearby hotel. The man's family assumed he had been killed.

Somehow I end up telling Lucas about how I wasn't near any of the buildings on the Tech campus where the shootings took place because I was off to a late start that morning, and attempted to jumpstart my day by working out.

"You were there? At Virginia Tech?" He asks.

"Well, no, not in any of those classrooms, but yes, on campus." For some reason, I feel it's okay for him to know a little piece of something that I hold like a frozen, weighted stone in my memory bank.

This is the first time I've seen him operate in a non-comical, somber capacity. Typically, he smiles effortlessly and constantly. I look directly into his face. He's not smiling.

I try to change the subject, to move away from this uncomfortable conversation. I was the one who mentioned it, but I don't want to discuss it. Especially not at a birthday party.

A saxophonist begins to serenade the group, and eventually leads us in a performance of "happy birthday."

After the song, Lucas excuses himself to find the restroom and I notice that Tess is missing. I find her at the bar, flirting with the bartender.

"Lucas is fantastic" she gushes. "A bit of a ham, but you know I love that," she says.

Lucas joins us at the bar, and randomly tells me about his favorite episode of Animal Planet. He elaborately explains how a couple times a year, a species of sardines embarks on a migration journey. Dolphins cleverly steer them into balls of confused sardines and begin to feast. Next, birds SWOOP from the sky to capitalize on the sardine buffet. Laughing Lucas gives all of these animals dialog and distinct voices, and transforms this biology lesson into a dramatic and highly entertaining story.

"You know what you could do?" I inquire.

"No, what?" he asks.

"You could have a show where you teach children science, but you tell it as a series of stories, with voices, and humor… you make it fun, and therefore memorable. I think that could be your niche."

"I never considered that" he says.

"Well, I think you'd be great at it."

We look up and spot the bartender serving Tess complimentary brochette and filling her glass with champagne as she smiles coyly.

"Your friends are quite the characters," he says.

Look who's talking, I think.

"When I first arrived here, Tess sort of socially adopted me. I've been very fortunate."

"I'm very good friends with the people I work with in the acting studio," he says and then continues, "What I mean is, that I've found a family here, too."

Eventually the party starts to break up and Tess announces that everyone is invited to attend a pregame at her apartment and then take a limo to a club. She adds that she, however, does NOT need to pregame. We can all tell.

I turn to Lucas and ask if he minds giving me a ride home.

In the car, he asks, "Would you tell me about your parents?"

"What do you want to know?"

"How did they meet?" he asks.

We exchange the stories of how our parents met and almost miss my exit.

As we pull into my driveway, I invite him to join me for the Down Town Art Walk on Thursday. We agree to attend the Art Walk and then make an appearance at a chocolate fundraising event organized by one of his friends.

"Thank you for driving me home, and thank you for coming tonight. I had a really great time, and Tess really enjoyed meeting you. She told me so," I say.

"I had a great time too, and your friends are great," he replies.

I look at his face, illuminated by the driveway light. I want to kiss him. I think of the other men, I think of the book, I reach for the door handle- and I don't. I don't kiss him.

A good night kiss would have been appropriate, even called for. I know we both considered it. I wonder if in my attempt to protect him, I offended him. I wonder if sometimes a kiss is merely a way to test if you really like someone, a chance to try something and see if, or how much, you like it.

Since I didn't drive, I don't have my keys. I ring the doorbell and wait for my aunt to let me in. As I turn to close the door behind me I see his car lights in the street. He' still there, waiting to make sure I get in safely.

"Well?" Aunt Ellen asks.

"Well, I thought about kissing him, but stopped myself because of the other men. It just seems wrong," I say.

"If you felt like you wanted to kiss him, you should have kissed him. There's nothing wrong with that."

"I don't know anymore," I mutter, and head to my bedroom. I call Woodlands Will to see if he's still up for a rendezvous. It's almost 9 pm, so I suggest ice cream, my treat.

Will drives the few miles from his house to mine. He greets me at the front door and introduces himself to aunt Ellen. I can tell she's thinking about how cute he is.

Once we're at the restaurant and seated with our ice cream, I tell Will everything. I tell him everything I've wanted to tell all the men I've met. I tell him how many men I've met and that I want to write a book. I tell him that I believe this story is remarkable and that the fact that it's not a story is also remarkable. I tell him I want to include the actual messages these men have sent me, because that is what will make the book authentic and prove that these men are not characters, but real people. This isn't just about me anymore, it's about illustrating to other women that great guys are out there, and further, that they are on sites like Match.com. I tell him I don't know how or when to tell the men, or how to ask their permission to print their words.

I explain it all, rapidly and completely. My eyes are on the brink of welling up with tears. He listens, carefully and without judgment.

Then he responds, "First of all, I don't mind if you include the messages I sent you or the conversation from our date. I have nothing to hide and I'm comfortable with who I am. Now, as a writer myself, let me give you a few pointers. You can change certain details in a scene but still create the same effect and emotions. You have to consider what's essential and what's important. The things that aren't essential are the things you can change to protect the identity of the men. And, the dates alone aren't what's interesting; but rather, the 'guts' of the story really lie in your reaction to the dates. [I make a note to myself here to further take the microscope off the men, and redirect onto myself.] I would suggest you first write the book, then, you meet with each of the men you want to quote. You print the excerpts about them and tell them that you'd like them to read those parts but that you can't let them read the book in it's entirety until the other men give their consent. That way, they don't have to wonder how they will be portrayed."

I reply, "Well, the men that are main characters in this book will be portrayed very respectfully, because I wouldn't go on more than one date with someone I didn't respect. For example, I'd like to include the funny messages you sent me. Your real words illustrate your humor and personality better than I ever could."

"Would you consider putting my phone number at the end of the book then?" He jokes.

(He doesn't know I've considered that already.)

I continue, "I'm worried that these men will be hurt or angry when they discover how many dates I've been on in such a short amount of time. Or injured by the knowledge that although I've 'found them', I continue to keep searching. In fact, I'm so torn up about it, that I've worn a hole not in my heart, but on my upper ribcage. Literally. The best way for me to clear my head is to run, and my head feels so bewildering cloudy these days that I've been running A LOT. The accumulation of millions of minutes spent with a damp jog bra chaffing against my skin has literally created an abrasion."

I'm not sure why I just told him that.

"Well, that's kind of gross," he says.

"I know, sorry" I apologize. I should probably reserve that level of gory detail for the friends I've known for years, not days…

He continues, "Pardon the expression, but until someone 'puts a ring on your finger' there's nothing saying you can't see other people. Also, for all you know the men could be going on dates with other women."

"I hope they are," I declare. And then, "I'm sorry, I'm a mess, you must think I'm insane."

"No, I think what you're doing is incredible. You have passion. Lots of people have big ideas and things they want to do in their lives but they don't follow through because they're too scared or because they're making excuses about why they can't. You're not. You're not telling yourself that you've never written a book and don't know how; you're just doing it. You believe in it. You believe in your story, your idea, and your passion."

I immediately grab a napkin from the table and start jotting down notes about the little inspirational speech he just delivered. He watches me in amusement, and starts laughing.

"It's okay with you if I include this in my book, right?" I ask.

"Of course" he says.

"What's the Star Wars character? Yoda? I feel like I'm the young Jedi writer and you are Yoda!" I say.

He laughs and then jokes, "Perhaps I need to gain one-hundred pounds and let you rub my belly?"

"Absolutely" I say.

I realize how much I am enjoying spending time with Will in such pressure-less setting. I find myself hoping, sincerely, that he will be a "prominent character" in my life, but not in the way that I initially considered. I'd really like to be his friend, for the long run. Maybe my feelings could even bloom into something more in future years, you never know. All I know is that he's a great guy and that he's generous with his knowledge, his advice, and his friendship.

Once my awkward confession is out of the way, I ask him about his day. I know he had planned to spend it with a real-estate agent, looking for a condo to buy.

"Well, I've seen many apartments, and overall, I've seen everything I've wanted, so I know it's out there, but I just haven't yet found it all in one single apartment." He says.

"It's like Match.com!!!! You meet all these people who have bits and pieces of everything you want and need, so you keep looking for that one person who could be your 'all'" I exclaim.

He laughs, and replies, "Exactly! Shopping for people, shopping for apartments. Seeking a woman between twenty and thirty who lives within thirty miles of LA and enjoys long walks on the beach... translates to seeking a condo between ten and twenty years old located within thirty miles of LA with a great view of the beach..."

We both burst out laughing.

Before talking with Will tonight, I felt like I was going to throw up, or cry or both (simultaneously). And now, Will has me laughing. From an objective perspective, he's not the 'winner' in the contest for my heart. He didn't make it to a second date which makes him appear as the loser. But, after meeting me, I think he realized this wasn't a competition he wanted to win. And, if you really look at it objectively, at the end of the day, who am I treating to ice cream? Woodlands Will.

He didn't win my heart and I didn't win his. At least not right off the bat. But, from where I'm sitting right now, we're both winning.

Maybe friendship IS the 'gotta have it' relationship.

On the drive back to my house, he gets lost. We're only a few miles from where he lives; it seems we share the same ludicrously poor sense of direction. I smile. I find amusement in discovering the things people may have in common, but don't broadcast on their profiles. Once he gets the GPS going and can focus on conversation, I ask him if he believes in love at first sight and if he's ever been in love.

He responds, "Yes. To both. But it wasn't mutual. I met her at a party and she was with someone. But that feeling was there. That feeling where you start talking really fast and the people around you think you're crazy because you sound like hummingbirds. That feeling where you know you're not going to be able to stop thinking about them, and all you do is think about when you'll get to see them next."

His words well up inside me. The way he described it is precisely accurate. I tell him so and take out my pen to jot the word "hummingbirds" on my hand.

He sees my scribbles and says, "If you come up with an animal that works better feel free to fudge it, I don't know if that's exactly the right bird…"

"It's exactly right," I say.

I pause a moment, and then ask him, "So, what are YOU looking for?"

"I'm not specifically looking for a relationship, or a hook-up, or even love. I'm looking for a grand connection with someone. Just a grand connection."

"Me too. But I think that's how I define love- a 'grand connection.'"

He drops me off and I thank him, sincerely, for everything. I tell him that I'd like it if he came with me to one of my friends' parties and that if he ever needs to get something off his chest, or just wants someone to listen and eat soft-serve with, I hope he'll call me. I mean it.

When I walk through the front door, aunt Ellen greets me and prods, "Well, are you in love with him?"

"No, we're just friends."

"But he's so good looking!" She exclaims.

"Yes, he is, but I'm grateful to have him as a friend and don't want to be more than friends with him."

"I want to be more than friends with him!" She whines.

I laugh and retreat to my bedroom to write down his words of wisdom while they are still in reach and resonating in my head.

At 4 am, I put my Macbook to sleep so that I can put my brain to rest as well.

Once the screen goes blank, it reflects the face of a little girl with whom I am intimately familiar.

Her eyes look inquisitive, but tired.

I squint, and find a young woman.

I'm not sure what she's looking for.

PASTA, RELATIONSHIPS, AND BOILING POINTS

Finally, the rain ceases. For the first time in days, I can open the shutters and glass panes of my bedroom windows. While I clean up the mess I left yesterday (in my haste to select an outfit for Tess's party, I left a tornado in my wake), I dial Charlie.

He's the one who left me both more open to love than I knew possible AND terribly wounded in his wake. Perhaps I should first attempt to fully understand why the most meaningful relationship of my past ultimately fell to pieces, before embarking on a new one.

Charlie answers on the second ring, "Rachel?!"

"Hello Charlie, wow, it's great to hear your voice. Listen, I know it's been awhile since we've spoken, but I really need your help with something," I say.

"Oh, okay. Anything. How can I help?" he asks.

I tell him about my recent dating experiences and that I want to write a book about it. I explain, "In order to truly unlock my character, I need to better understand why you and I broke up. At the time of the actual breakup, I was trying so hard to be angry because I was so unbearably hurt. I really wasn't able to logically process our descent. Now that it's been years, and we've both moved on, I'd like to know not only what you think caused our relationship to go sour, but also, how dating me affected what you looked for in subsequent relationships."

He replies, "I haven't thought about this in years. Let me put some time into thinking it over. I promise to call back in a few days. Is that okay?"

"Of course." I say, "Take your time and let me know when you're ready to talk about it."

"Will do. Speak to you soon," he says.

"Okay, thank you… take care…"

I hang up and I realize I've wanted to ask this for a while now.

My questions for him aren't pointed or accusing. I want answers for my own understanding and peace of mind. I think sometimes the end of a relationship is so poignant, so difficult, that in the months/years that follow, the aftermath is what stands as most memorable. I'm ready to revisit, and hopefully finally understand, the moments and sentiments that lead up to that ending.

My Charlie thoughts are interrupted by a text message from Med-School Mat:

"Such a nice day! I hope you're out enjoying it."

Although I had intended on taking a break from running today, the warm air filtering in from the open windows combined with Med-School Mat's message, inspires me to throw on my running clothes and bolt for the door. I want to be outside.

The suburban house-lined streets are quaint and almost artificial looking. I can't discern many visual changes on these streets from run to run, or even month to month. This is partly because not much changes in the Valley and also because of California's "endless summer." When I first moved here, the lack of obvious seasonal changes really confused me and played tricks on my internal clock.

In mid September, I had lived in California for almost four months, but from looking around, it seemed as though nothing had changed. The trees were still green, the leaves still hanging heavy on the branches. There were no wood-burning smells drifting into the streets, hinting of the first few of the fall season's early evening fires. I could still run before anyone else was awake, wearing only light cotton leggings and a t-shirt.

Without visual hints of progression from the natural world around me, I felt as though time was standing still. It was unsettling. I called Tess and asked her if we could get away from LA for a day, drive somewhere to see evidence that summer was over and that autumn had arrived. I suggested we orchestrate an apple-picking trip.

"Rachel, no one in LA goes apple picking," she said.

I pleaded, "I just need to wander through an orchard. I'm craving the burnt orange color that the leaves should be by now and the taste of hot apple cider."

For the first time, I understood what my father meant when he said he could never leave the east coast, because he would miss the seasons.

By November, the foliage finally began to transform, let go from the burly tree limbs, and decay. And, in the mean time, Tess found a nearby fall festival with a corn maze and pumpkin patch to get me through my first experience with California's strangely subtle seasonal transitions.

Today, I am keenly aware that winter is in full swing and that spring is gaining on me. The clues are everywhere. I discover an entire cul-de-sac filled with swooping trees that seem to droop from the weight of an excessive number of white blossoms. The previous week's unremitting rain has pounded nearly half of the petals out of the arms of the trees, and down onto the street.

The bright white of the silky flowers is exquisite and shocking against the black of the rough pavement, and the image shouts of change, succession, and transformation.

Even if these blossoms weren't ready to fall, the insistent sky with bullying rain clouds hurried them along, and gave them no choice.

The premature flight of the flowers and the startling indication of natural growth seems fitting for this month. Since joining Match.com, it has seemed as though time has moved much more quickly than it did in the previous months. I realize this is partly my fault. Any project I take on, I jump into with both feet, and invest myself fully. Therefore, while most young women might start off with one date every other week, I sought one date every night. I've been pulled along under a magnetic wave of fast-forward. In the realm of my social life, more has happened in the past two weeks than in the past six months combined.

I have to stop and walk for a few minutes, to catch my breath. Without realizing it, I had begun to run a bit too quickly. Once I stop, I have trouble regaining momentum and end up walking the rest of the way home.

At this slowed pace, I'm aware of even more details and clues to spring, too many to observe them all. I'm grateful the seasons are cyclic, and that next year, and future years, will offer a second chance.

Once I return to my desk chair, I reluctantly check my Match-box. I make a conscious decision to stop responding to messages from new men. There are enough on the horizon. I've learned that sometimes even sending a polite "decline" message ignites a string of further messages, and requests for reconsideration.

I think of the fenced yards I sometimes run past, where dogs bark at me from between the wood planks. When it's just one fenced-in pet howling at me, I can handle it. When I happen upon a string of homes in a row, each with fenced yard containing a loud and aggressive canine, it exhausts me.

Usually, a dog will start yelping at me when I approach the corner of his lot, and then run alongside me, barking as loudly as he can, until I pass his property line. As soon as I cross the border, off of his territory, the next yard's dog will pick up loudly yelping alongside me where the previous animal left off. I can only run past so many in a row before I have to avoid that particular street altogether. My Matchbox is becoming a street I'm tempted to avoid altogether.

Today, however, I am thankful I checked in, because I find a message from Adventure Alex:

Hey!

I wanted to tell you that I really enjoyed our conversation last night. You have a lot of energy and you're very passionate. I really hope we can get together again soon. Hope you're having a great Saturday!

Alex

I respond, proposing we go to Cal State to hear the LA Phil on Wednesday. There's another installation of the "Neighborhood Concerts" series that I went to with Similarities Steve. I want a second chance to hear the LA Phil play, but in the company of someone else who is just as enthused for this specific chance.

Alex responds:

As far as Wednesday, my night is yours. You're welcome to come to the West side but I could also meet in the Valley if it's too much trouble. I would love to show you this part of town since you mentioned you'll eventually be moving here. Better to get a jump-start on all the fine eateries we have to offer, etc.

I would love to see the LA Phil! I saw them perform Handel's "Messiah" just before Christmas and it was amazing.

Cheers!

Alex

I send him the link to the event, tell him I've already called to reserve tickets, and suggest we meet at his apartment as I will already be in Santa Monica (his part of town) on Wednesday. I send him a google map showing the location of my house (The Valley), my work (Santa Monica), his house (West side), and the event venue (east of LA) so that we can plan accordingly. After six months of LA traffic (neither predictable nor enjoyable), I've learned to pre-choreograph transportation to ensure efficiency. I don't want to spend the majority of the hours of my day on the highways, just as much as I don't want to spend them on the internet.

He replies:

The program looks amazing! It'll be so nice to hear all three parts of the "Marriage of Figaro" after recently seeing "The Barber of Seville."

Wow. I don't know if someone told you the way to my heart, but including an annotated map in your email was a step in the right direction.

That sounds like a great plan. I even like the geographic efficiency of it. You are more than welcome to leave your car at my house and I love driving/would be happy to drive.

If anything comes up between now and then, or if you just want to chat, feel free to give me a call.

Hope all is well,

Cheers!

Alex

I reply:

Great! THANK you for driving!

And, I'll let you choose the place for dinner!

...and while I'm at it... perhaps I should also mention that on this relaxing Sunday I am wearing a super soft bedroom robe- paired with green and white argyle knee socks. Yes, I'm borderline obsessed with knee socks. And, I also went through a kilt phase...but it was WAY back in elementary school (and it was because my grandfather brought one back for me from his travels and I thought that was VERY COOL). Hahahahaha... hope you aren't spooked. ;)

Ok... enough for now. Feel free to share a strange/surprising- or better yet, an equally embarrassing personal tid-bit.

:-)

RL

He responds:

Have I told you how your emails make me smile/laugh out loud every time I read them? It's amazing.

So, I'm trying to picture you in a plush robe and argyle knee socks.

Again... Smile on my face. I don't know that I have any quirky dressing habits. Although... I really struggle with wearing sandals. I don't really know why. I think it's just a preparedness thing. It's like I always want to be ready for action and I don't feel like I can get up and go if I'm wearing sandals.

Also, I love ties. You know how ties are kind of considered a cliché gift for a guy and nobody wants to resort to buying you a tie? It kills me because ties are some of my favorite gifts!

So, does that mean you don't have any of your kilts anymore? I'd love to see them if you still had them around ;)

Alex

As I finish reading his last message, I'm grinning merrily at the computer screen. I am incredibly turned on by his messages, perhaps even more so than I am to him in the flesh. I start to worry that maybe I'm falling for Alex the writer, the fictional, romantic pen-pal character, not the actual person. Is it possible to perceive more chemistry from a string of black 11 point Helvetica letters, than with a dashing young man?

Will Adventure Alex and I sustain this astonishing string of notes in the long run? Are these messages destined to be the first ten or so cherished letters of what will grow to be a much larger collection? Are the letters we exchanged while he was in Kenya the first installment of the correspondence with my future fiancé, which we will print and frame for the guests to view and savor at our engagement party? Will our written words to each other prove to be artifacts that lead up to an occasion that neither one of us could currently predict or even suggest with any certainty or even probability? Or will the emails eventually be reduced to nothing more than a series of romance letters from a long lost could-have-been, accumulating dust in an attic somewhere because the words on the page didn't correlate exactly to the shell and flesh of the author who penned them?

Uncle Carl starts hollering my name. I bolt to the kitchen and find aunt Ellen buzzing around the kitchen, fussing over a pot of boiling water.

Uncle Carl is standing at the edge of the island, with the keys to his Mercedes in one hand, and a bottle of wine in the other. He looks at me, and pleads, "Will you please tell your auntie here that you are capable of successfully creating a batch of pasta so that we can leave for our Super Bowl party?"

I give him my "crim-a-ninny we go through this with her over and over again" look, and then say "Aunt Ellen, I've got this, you and uncle Carl can go to the party now!"

She begins to search for a timer (I tell her repeatedly I will sit at the counter and watch the oven clock), rummaging through her purse for a pair of glasses to read the instructions on the back of the pasta package aloud to me (I tell her repeatedly I've made pasta before), and then tells me multiple, multiple times, that when pouring the hot water into the strainer I must pour AWAY from my body (I tell her repeatedly that I'm 23, not 11).

Finally, uncle Carl exclaims, "ELLEN she builds GODDAMN houses, she can boil a freakin pot of pasta!"

She continues to scurry around the kitchen, and replies, "Well, I don't know that she CAN boil a pot of pasta and I also know that I can't build houses."

He replies, "You aren't making sense and you can't make a pot of pasta either! At least not today! NOW GET IN THE CAR!"

I plead with her, "Please aunt Ellen, just go to your party already! I PROMISE I'm completely capable. Everything is under control! If you don't leave soon, uncle Carl is going to start guzzling the wine bottle under his arm."

She replies, "BUT the pasta must be made, and ready, and PERFECT for the grandchildren incase they stop by after their baseball games!"

It's obvious to both uncle Carl and me that she is not going to leave until she's certain that the pasta will be boiled and prepared properly. Further, it's obvious that they will be late to their party.

Uncle Carl turns to me, points to the embroidered brand label on the chest of his collared sweater, and shouts, "See here? This should be a GOLD STAR! Do you see what I put up with?!"

I roll my eyes and tell him to enjoy the game. He storms out the door and waits in the car for her. At long last, she makes a start to leave. As I close the door behind her and turn the knob to lock it, I hear her cry "Oh! Wait! I was supposed to bring cheese!"

I let her in and run ahead of her to the refrigerator and start filling a container with whatever random assortment of cheeses I can quickly get my hands on. On her second attempt, she successfully makes it completely (and finally) out the door, with packages of brie and chevre falling out of her tote and rolling into the flower beds. At this point, uncle Carl has waited fifteen minutes for her inside the house and twelve minutes in his car. What's even more ludicrous is that they repeat this scenario, or a scenario very similar to the one that just played out, at least three times per week.

Our entire family and all of our friends know that aunt Ellen has the generosity and patience of a nun. What they don't know, is that uncle Carl has that of a saint. Although from watching this string of events pan out many times per week, I've realized that secretly he might really take pleasure in waiting for her. It's his way of waiting on her. It's his way of loving her.

Yes, I think it is love, or maybe it's sainthood, or perhaps a bit of both.

MIRACULOUS SCIENCE
OR SCIENTIFIC MIRACLES

I set out on a casual morning run with no predetermined route; content to go where my feet lead me. I'm not surprised to find my legs propelling me towards the gated orange grove two miles from my house. I still remember the exact morning, a few weeks after I moved to California, that I discovered the hidden break in the boundary, along the backside of the property, narrow and veiled by the thick summer foliage. There is a large entrance off of the main road but on the weekends the heavy, iron gate is closed. This tiny, unidentified threshold gives me access to the orchard while others are locked out.

With only my footsteps for company, and on rare occasions a silent, lone groundskeeper, I run up and down the rows of orange trees in quiet reverence. Even on steamy August mornings, I inhale not the salty smell of my own skin, but the refreshing cologne of citrus.

During the month of September, I have to be careful where I let my feet land, so as not to break an ankle on a fallen or mulch-hidden fruit. The produce is so abundant that when September slowly bows to November, there are more oranges than the grounds keeper can possibly collect or sell. Since I visit the patch almost daily, I notice when certain larger oranges begin to rot. Some oranges are so ripe, that they beg to be eaten immediately. They cannot wait to be found, collected, and stored for sale. They are so ideally primed, so brimming with sugared juices and readiness, that if the fleeting window of opportunity for eating them is missed, it will be gone forever, leaving only a browning, putrid core in its wake.

The groundskeeper understands this, and can tell that I do too. We never exchange a word, but often watch each other from the outermost edges of our periphery.

On one of those festively ripe mornings when all the paths were carpeted with fallen fruit, I had to search to see even small patches of dirt and therefore had to slow my pace to almost a walk. I bent down and picked up one of the oranges, and, for the first time, the groundskeeper and I made eye contact. Throughout the orchard, there are clearly written signs warning against touching, picking, or taking the fruit. I had read these signs, but wasn't thinking of them in this moment.

I let my focus remain on the groundskeeper, and my eyes rested on his face. I scanned his dove-white hair and sun-leathered neck and forehead, which appeared to be compartmentalized into various zones by branch-like wrinkles. He didn't smile, nor did he nod. But, without the slightest discernable movement or intentional expression, he gave me permission.

From that morning on, it became my routine to run to the orchard, select the most ripe, eager fruit I could find, pick it up, run home with the heavy orb in hand, and feast on this incredible gift of my own finding.

The orchard became a personal, intensely private retreat. Even on the days the groundskeeper and I were both present, we didn't intrude on each other's individual consciousness. For the most part and most of the time, we were undisturbed and even on the most primal level, unaware of each other's presence.

One weekend morning, a tour bus of senior citizens from a nearby assisted living community parked at the grove. The tree-lined rows became littered with people gaily chatting and meandering. In the context of my found haven, my place of refuge, I perceived them as intruders.

Maybe this is a clue as to how I'll know if and when I love someone. Maybe being in love means that you want to invite them into your most personal, most secret, garden. Maybe being in love means that that guarded place in your mind, located as far as possible from the lobes of logic and reason, the delicate, precious, and sacred sanctuary, becomes receptive and inviting to someone else.

Maybe what I'm looking for is someone that I'd want to show this grove to. Maybe I'm searching for someone whose presence alone has the ability to enhance even my most independent, private moments and pleasures.

We all have activities in which we find personal joy, and therefore safeguard from others. For me, it's running. Usually, I don't run with other people. I prefer to run alone. Running is my time to focus inward, on myself, dissecting my own thoughts and ideas.

Hillary, my best friend at Virginia Tech, watched my love of running develop over our collegiate years. I remember the very first time I ran for an entire hour. As my watch display turned from fifty-six minutes to fifty-seven, I realized I was about to achieve an individual milestone. My breathing became labored and I had to fight back tears. My reaction was threatening my ability to actually reach my goal so I made an effort to push the processing thoughts out of my head and just RUN along the white fence of the campus golf course and up the hill to the sorority house.

Like am Olympian returning home with gold medal in hand, I made my way to Hillary's room.

"What's the matter?!" she asked, searching my tear streaked face.

"I just ran for an entire hour. I didn't know I had it in me to do that. It's taken so long to get here, and I did it. Like my parents, like my siblings, like you... now I really feel like a runner." I explained.

In hindsight, I know exactly why, before stretching or even showering, I went straight to her room. I had just experienced something that I found personally extraordinary, and wanted to share it with someone. I didn't have a boyfriend during that time, and was glad I had such an amazing best friend with whom I could celebrate these sorts of achievements. I think in many ways that's what people want when they say they want love. They want to have someone to witness their most significant instances, both the bad and the good. Throughout my life, I've been blessed with best friends with whom I shared a distinct type of love. The type of love where you know each catty argument will end in laughs, that the dreams and expectations you have for them may exceed those they have for themselves, and that any man who breaks their hearts… is a dead man.

When Hillary's sophomore-year boyfriend had too many drinks and offended me at a bar, Hillary came to my defense, and announced, loudly, "I am POSITIVE that Rachel WILL be in my wedding. However, as far as YOU are concerned, the jury is still out!"

I still consider myself new to California, and I'm painfully aware that those types of friendship are really a unique form of love and take time to build. I believe Tess and I are slowly cultivating that sort of friendship. However, for someone as dependent on both giving and receiving love as I am, it's very difficult to have patience.

So, maybe I know more about love than I realize. But, the type of love I've had for most of my life is different than the form I'm looking for now. I think as we grow up, the type of love we crave, changes. Somewhere along the way, the unconditional love from our parents, the steadfast love from our friends, and even the love we sense from doing the things that bring us the most joy, become insufficient. We grow to want more. To want a different and new breed of love. To find love in the form of a companion.

Maybe it's evolutionary. At a certain age, we're wired to begin to yearn for "a mate." This reality is what has ensured the survival of the human race. Maybe it's an animalistic and instinctual thought process of the brain. Pure science.

Or, maybe it's an intensely human hunger, that seeps from the heart, resulting in stories that may hinge on foundations of pure science, but indeed, are too, part miracle.

Wednesday, February 10

PHIL ME UP, TAKE TWO

I've been wondering a lot lately about how it's possible that I've met so many great guys yet still don't know if any of them is the right guy for me. How could I NOT know? Especially when I've "known at first sight" before.

Or maybe, just because I've experienced love at first sight before, doesn't mean it will happen that way again. I'm not the same person I was then. Perhaps, on some level, a part of me knows that what bruised me as a child could potentially break bone now that I'm an adult. I'm having the whole "it's not you, it's me" talk, with myself. Conceivably it's not that these guys aren't worthy of "fireworks," but rather, at this point my skin has healed (from love burns) and grown back so thick that it's hard for me to feel their heat.

Maybe, I'm not as receptive to love as I once was, or worse, critical of any potential source of it. I make a mental note to attempt to be more "receptive" during my date with Adventure Alex tonight.

After working in Santa Monica all day, I drive to Alex's so we can travel together to the auditorium at California State University. Days ago, when I tried to call and reserve tickets; they were already sold out. Hopefully, we can get there early and fill the seats of those who no-show.

Once we're on our way Alex asks, "What type of music do you listen to?"

"Lady GAGA but only for running...Augustana, The Fray, Chemical Romance...MIKA...but also Billy Joel and eighties music, what about you?" I ask.

"Well, you know I came from a small town, and all anyone ever listened to was country. One day I found an old dusty box of records. I spent about an hour figuring out how to play them, and once I did, I was hooked on Classic Rock. I would sneak out that box all the time to listen to the records. My favorite was one by Steve Miller Band." He says.

I reply, "'Jungle Love' was my dad's favorite song, we used to listen to it all the time!"

"Awesome! Here, my friend made me this eighties mix," he says, feeding the disc into the cd player.

By the time we arrive at the theatre (dancing about in the car to eighties hits), the line of people waiting for tickets (without reservations) is already snaking through the plaza.

"Wow this is a bummer," I whine.

"No it's not, I still think it will work out! Things tend to work out as they should." He reassures me.

A few minutes before the concert begins, we score a pair of tickets from a couple that decides not to stay for the show. We race into the concert hall like school children running at recess. During the concert, I am aware of him sitting beside me, enjoying the music.

After the show, he asks me what I want to do for dinner. It's late, and I still have a long drive back home to the Valley so I suggest someplace quick. Earlier, we had considered picking up McDonalds en-route to the concert so we could have an adventure eating while "camping out" in line for tickets. The timing ended up being too tight to even stop for fast food, so we simply drove straight to the concert without picking up dinner.

I suggest we still go to McDonalds. Jumping from a philharmonic concert to a fast-food chain is a bit strange, but I want to see how Alex "jives" in a random, fun, casual setting. I perceive his consistent charm as formal, so I want to get to know him better in a very informal setting. Formal is the LAST adjective that comes to mind when I think of McDonalds.

I realize that I'm digging to throw curve balls at him. In the past hour alone, I've made a point to mention that swimming in the ocean terrifies me (Alex loves to surf), that I almost failed the two structures courses required to earn my architecture degree (he effortlessly conquered all of the rigorous university mathematics courses necessary required in his curriculum), that I don't like "saucy foods" (in response to the fact that he LOVES Asian cuisine), AND, that yes, although I did complete two-half marathons, I don't intend to run many in the future, if any (in response to finding out that like my father, he was once a competitive triathlete).

Perhaps I'm initiating little attempts of sabotage because of my hunch that I could end up really falling for him. Since things could go far, I want to put a stop to it now if there's something about me that would guarantee it doesn't.

I want to lay all my cards on the table.

Well, all my cards except for those I'm hiding in my back pocket, bearing the faces of other men (Laughing Lucas my Jokester, Med-School Mat my Academic Ace, and Older Oliver, my aged yet perfect ten). If they knew of each other would they call "game-over" or worse, "War"? I look into the face of Adventure Alex, the King in front of me. Am I becoming the queen of hearts? Is the heart a muscle just like any other in the human body, which grows stronger the more you stretch and strain it?

By forcing my heart to inflate large enough to hold so many men at once, am I conditioning it as I did while training for my first half marathon, to achieve new levels of vitality?

Or, am I setting myself up for Cardiac Arrest?

I look at the hospital-like florescent lighting above, the grease covered french-fries on the plastic tray between us, and the carefully hung business jacket behind him.

I laugh, and remark, "This is bizarre, but FANTASTIC. Earlier we heard the LA Phil, and now, we are in a vinyl-covered McDonald's booth eating un-artistic, un-sophisticated food out of paper bags, under bad lighting."

He replies, "I'm pretty sure taking a girl to McDonalds for date two is a major crime, yet this is pretty spectacular- it works."

"Yes, it does. This is perfect. And, honestly, I will never turn down a McDonalds date because I am in LOVE with their soft-serve. They even have the dedicated soft-serve places beat. McDonalds makes the CREAMIEST soft-serve. Amazing."

Alex chimes in, "Agreed. It's definitely the best. I ate my fair share of McDonalds in college. The dollar menu kept me from literally being a 'starving college student'. It's certainly the best bang for your buck."

A drunkard wanders into the restaurant and has a one-sided conversation with a trash receptacle.

Alex and I look at each other searchingly. "Life is funny, and strange sometimes," I say.

"Yes it is." He says, smiling.

As he finishes his ice cream, he leans forward and whispers, "You're fun."

I reply, loudly, "You're fun too!"

We drive back to his apartment so I can get my car. As we turn onto his street, he asks me if I know Topanga well (since I had mentioned driving through Topanga Canyon this morning en-route to work). I reply, "No, I don't know the area well, I'm always just passing through it. It's a lot of winding curves and hidden, unpaved roads! But many times I have passed a sign reading 'Inn of the Seventh Ray', and finally looked it up online. It's a restaurant that has great reviews, and the ambiance seems remarkable. Hopefully, one day I'll be able to check it out," I say.

He flashes a big smile my way and reveals, "I have reservations for 8 pm this Sunday, at Inn of the Seventh Ray." And then he asks, "Sunday is Valentine's Day, will you join me?"

Wait! How did he know I've wanted to go there? I didn't mention it before! This is too much to be coincidence!

He repeats his offer, calmly, "Can pick you up Sunday?"

I smile, blushing, and reply, "Absolutely."

Thursday, February 11

WAKE UP CALL

Charlie calls, as promised, to discuss the things we both tried not to remember. When my phone jumps with vibration, I'm still in bed and hardly alert. I slowly turn my head to look at my phone on the nightstand. It's level with my face and I can clearly see the glowing screen. Even though I expected it, the illuminated named of my ex-boyfriend is quite the jarring wake up call.

He begins, "First, I want to say that when I starting thinking back, I thought about a lot of really good times. Remember the time Extreme Home Makeover came to campus? And we worked on the construction of the house from dusk till dawn? And you filled your pockets with jellybeans to keep us energized into the morning? And our freshman year, when Pat McGee Band came to play a concert and you ran up to him, asked for an autograph, realized you didn't have any paper, and so you asked him to sign YOUR ARM?"

"Yes! And then later, you miraculously tracked him down and had him call my phone and serenade me! That was marvelous… yes of course I remember," I reply.

Charlie continues, "I also remember meeting you, and being so amazed at how much we had in common: architecture, interests, upbringings, suburbia, and we were both 'prepsters' trying to find our way in a HUGE university. When I met you, it was almost too obvious. We had so much in common it seemed as though it couldn't NOT work."

"Right, you were my Match-made in 'common', excuse the expression," I say.

Charlie laughs lightly, "It's the perfect expression. Anyways, as our relationship progressed, and I began to get a better hold on the campus, and on myself, and who I wanted to be, I realized I wanted to change and grow. You reinforced everything I had been, and I wanted to grow out of that. I wanted to go in a different direction. I didn't know what it was I wanted to be, but I knew I wanted to be different, that I wanted to evolve. When we arrived at college, we were each other's safe choice. You're right; it's hard to pinpoint exactly why we broke up. Neither one of us did anything to ruin it, we didn't cheat or anything of the sort. We just started to grow. In a new environment, surrounded by new people, we found mirrors of ourselves in each other and we clung to each other, immediately, instinctively, and held on. Somewhere along the way I decided I wanted to branch out, and to branch away. You, in some ways, held tight to the context in which you'd spent the previous years of your life. And somehow, I began to perceive you as a threat to my evolution. Our similarities at the beginning became our differences at the end. We didn't want to split, but we were splitting. We didn't decide we hated each other, or had wronged each other, we just started to split. As we grew, it just started to happen. That's the way I see it."

I reply, "Wow, I've been waiting a long time to hear all of that. I wanted to hear it sooner, but I wasn't ready. I couldn't have understood it. I couldn't have listened. You're right, from the moment I met you I knew we were alike, that you were a safe bet. You seemed familiar from the beginning, because personality wise, finding you was like finding another me, in a male shell. I had just graduated from a tiny boarding school and was finding my way at a huge university. It was new and different, and thrilling, but a bit intimidating. I wanted reassurance that I belonged there. I found exactly that, in you. Or exactly me, in you. Finding another "me" reinforced everything I was. You fortified my confidence. I felt twice as confident in the sea of strangers because with you by my side I felt "double." We made friends simultaneously and watched and encouraged each other in the process. We were so alike we even made friends in the same way, went to the same parties, socialized in the same circles. We took clues from each other, and bolstered each other. Even before we were dating, we were best friends, and already a 'we'. I never felt like I had to do anything alone my freshman year. I had you, this incredible underpinning of myself. I think that's why it was so difficult for me when we broke up. I perceived you as a part of me. I mistakenly thought you completed me, that in the separation I would somehow be left lacking. I've grown so much. I'm not looking for someone to complete me this time, just compliment me. And I'm glad that when things started to get ugly and we both recognized it, you were adamant about cutting all ties."

He replies, "You know how I am, no gray area- I only see in black and white."

I continue, "Right. Thank God. I would have dragged it on. No matter how apparent it was that we were growing apart, I was afraid of letting go. I couldn't have let go completely if you hadn't made that the only option. It's amazing to look back and be able to see it as it really was. It all seemed so foggy at the time."

"I hope what I said was helpful, was it?" He asks.

"Very much so, I'm going to go run when we hang up so I can clear my head and think about it further," I reply.

"What? You're going to go running to clear your head? When we were together you hated running. HATED it." He says.

I reply, "That's so weird because in this book, I think running comes off as one of the great loves of my life. And it is. I forgot that I used to detest it."

"You're not the same person you were," He says.

"No, I'm not" I say, and continue, "Do you think, back then we were in love? Really in love? Or infatuation? Or juvenile delusion?"

Charlie pauses, and then says, "I think the definition of love changes as you age. When you're fifteen you might really think you're in love with someone and then years later write it off as puppy love because by then you've experienced a different sort of love. BUT, when you were fifteen you FELT you were in LOVE. So, you WERE in love. It's a feeling. When we were dating, I felt 'in love'. I felt that I loved you. I know that I loved you." He says.

The events I've witnessed this month have proven his theory that there are different types of love that we experience at different times in our lives. I think of my father strutting about dressed as what my mother perceives as resembling a bladder infection and my uncle Carl waiting for aunt Ellen for the billionth time in their marriage. Each time, his temper rises just shy of boiling point, yet not once has he left without her. Our personal definitions of love may evolve as we age, but love perceived, no matter the age or circumstance, is indeed love.

"I loved you too," I reply.

He jumps in, "I just remembered the first time I told you… we were in…"

I pick up before he can continue, "my bedroom in Collegiate Suites, sophomore year. I know, I just remembered it the other day, and wrote about it. The first time you told me you loved me. I remember it, too."

Perhaps the fact that well fell for each other so fast is proof of how fleeting and fragile that love was, and therefore not sustainable nor meant for the long term. Perhaps it's evidence that we were just children, running recklessly, unaware that not all breaks are clean and therefore not all breaks can be fixed with colorful casts and without complications. We didn't know that hearts can be broken into shards and that reassembling the pieces can be more complicated than simply reconnecting two split halves.

Charlie explains, "I think we both grew a lot from it. From being in love and from the breakup. If love is the ultimate happiness, isn't an education about love more important than, say, 'Steel Structures 101' for example? In a way, thanks to each other, we had a complete education at Tech, an education not only about the practical and professional, but also about the personal and intimate."

If I've already taken "Love 101," how will the next round be different?

I tell Charlie about Adventure Alex. I explain that Alex is bright, handsome, funny, and charismatic. I divulge that I'm intrigued by Alex, although he and I don't have much in common and come from different backgrounds and geographic locations. We have opposite interests and talents. Or maybe the right word is complimentary. This is all new and I'm still figuring it out.

Charlie replies, "If I told you back then you'd be dating a boy with whom you had hardly anything in common would you believe me?"

I reply, "No, but I'm not looking to date myself again, thank you very much."

"Ha, OK, thanks" he laughs and says, "I told my girlfriend about your book and she thinks a lot of women will want to read it."

"Tell her thank you! I'm really excited about it. For so many reasons... Charlie?"

"Yes Rachel?"

"I'm so glad we're finally here."

"Me too."

As I hang up the phone and make a move for my running shoes, I notice I'm humming snippets of the heart-buildingly beautiful overture I heard last night with Alex.

Halfway through my run, sharp pains shoot up my leg. I feel my knees start to give and have to slow to a walk in order to prevent my body from making love to the concrete sidewalk.

I hear the plea, echoing in my limbs, and come to the following conclusion:

My mind, body, and soul are ready for me to return to a more sustainable pace. I need just that, some sort of "conclusion" to this dating chaos.

Back in my room, I stare blankly into my closet. I need to get dressed for work and then my date with Laughing Lucas but I can't for the life of me recall which outfits he's already seen. I have been on so many dates lately.

This has to stop.

I decide on fitted lavender jeans, a cream sweater, my gold pocket-watch necklace, and horse-hair ballerina flats. Does this outfit say "I'm 90% sure I like you, but I'm 90% sure I MIGHT like another man as well, so I want to spend time with you both to decide"? I hope so.

After work I meet Laughing Lucas at his house so that we can ride downtown together for the Art Walk. I realize I must be visibly stressed from my day at the office because Lucas's first words upon seeing me at his door are "Hey Lady, are you feeling alright?"

"Yes, just a long day at work," I reply. I don't reveal the reason I'm a bit behind at the office. In an effort to cram in so many dates, I've stopped working late and instead leave early to beat traffic.

Regardless of my stress level upon arrival at Lucas's house, after fifteen minutes in the car with him I forget all about my office woes. By the time we park downtown my cheeks are slightly pained from smiling. His humor is a gift, and I'm grateful he's so generous with it.

Hand in hand, we head towards the streets filled with free spirited Angelenos, crawling traffic, dirty sidewalks, and wacky galleries. The composition of people, art, and cars is visually overwhelming. I don't know where to look first. Lucas walks beside me, amused by my reactions to the spectacles surrounding us on each block. I'm a visual person; I notice and observe everything in minute detail. In cities, there is more to survey than my eyes can handle. It's just too much. I love it.

Every sparse and cavernous loft-gallery we walk through makes me wonder how I would shape the space if given the chance. Every tall residential tower has me imagining which window would be mine. We make a game of it, just as we did with the round of I-spy while stuck in traffic en-route to our date at the Hammer.

"Okay, on this building would you choose that green glowing one?" Lucas asks, pointing his arm up towards an illuminated pane high above the intersection.

"No! I'd choose the one on the corner with the white lights strung carefully along the tiny white balcony!" I tease.

We discover that I intentionally steer clear of people walking their dogs along the sidewalk while Lucas, on the other hand, runs towards canines, squealing "PUUUPPPPYY." We also have opposing tastes in art. We enter one gallery where there's a musician playing an instrument I can't recognize. Lucas stands mesmerized while I weave ahead through the crowds and find myself in a small walled-in space, surrounded by a set of silk-screens on scrap plywood. These pieces hold my attention for quite awhile (and my heart for longer). While Lucas stands near the entrance with the gathering crowd entranced by the music, I savor the near solitude I've found in this small alcove. I appreciate the chance to study these artistic compositions alone, save for the company of the artist.

Lucas and I continuously wander off independently, and then reunite to share our reactions. We revel in our shared appreciation for inspiration and art in all its forms. A few times, I stop to take a photograph of something on the street, and look up to find him pulled far ahead by the swarms of people, standing, looking back at me and motioning his arm in a goofy wave to catch the attention of my searching eyes.

After conquering a few blocks of the Art Walk, we head to Lucas's friend's Champagne and Chocolate fundraising party (benefitting the Korea Town youth organizations). The event is on the outdoor rooftop-lounge of an upscale apartment building. There are rows of cabanas lit by votive candles, and the tables are decorated with stacked trays of beautifully designed artisan and gourmet chocolates and truffles.

After visiting every cabana (I like to make sure I don't miss anything, so our first ten minutes at the party is a bit like trick or treating as we pop into each cabana to take a peak), we settle down in one with praline milk chocolates. "You're very independent, aren't you?" Lucas asks.

"Yes, but I still depend on others. I mean, I joined a sorority for heaven's sake- and LOVED it. I feel compelled to nurture those around me, and consequently find myself surrounded by people that nurture me in return," I reply.

"Right, well, I meant in the self-sufficient sense," he replies.

"Oh. I derive a lot of my self worth from my self-sufficiency. Take moving out of my aunt and uncle's house. No matter what, full time job or not, I will get my own apartment within my first year of living in California. And I will fund the move entirely on my own. It's not that my parents aren't willing to help me, it's that I want to be self sufficient," I say.

"You do give off the 'I can take care of myself vibe'. It's almost un-girly which is funny considering how feminine you are." He smiles.

I look down at my ballet flats and smile in return.

"Yes, but really I'm a big contradiction of sorts. In high school and college, I participated in many internships and always intentionally erred on the androgynous side with my attire. Blazers, straight trousers, and gender-neutral clothing- a masculine structured jacket scaled down to a woman's frame. I didn't want anyone to ever wonder if I was able to hold my own. But, too, I appreciate when a man opens the door for me and offers his jacket. It's chivalrous."

"Hahahaha… good!" He replies.

"I'm working really hard these days towards self-sufficiency, I think about it every day. I'm just incredibly goal-oriented, and it's my current goal," I explain.

"Well you're on the cusp. So close. I remember being there. It's pretty cool when you finally cross over. I don't mean that in a condescending way. I only mean that I get it; I remember it. The anticipatory excitement."

"Yes, but I have to remind myself that this side of the cusp is pretty great, too. I get easily caught up in it all, I have to remember that even though I'm not exactly where I want to be, where I am now… is spectacular. You seem like you remember to recognize that you're happy. Do you think you're happier than most people? You seem happier. A lot happier," I say.

"I think I am. But I wasn't always. I had horrific migraines as a child from stressing all the time, and it was my mother who helped me understand that I was letting life and external forces negatively affect me. Thanks to her, something clicked. No more migraines, and I'm happy when I want to be happy, which is most of the time."

The party starts to die down, and Lucas's friend, the hostess of the event, comes to our cabana. She greets Lucas warmly. Lucas introduces me and she greets me just as warmly. She tells him that she wants to throw an event like this for one of his acting groups. They discuss the details and then we bid farewell and head to Lucas's car.

Once he safely returns me to my car, I thank him for another fantastically fun evening, and then I say, slowly, "Listen, I want to tell you something, and it's against the advice of my girlfriends, and I sincerely believe that telling you is selfish, because I'm aware that these words aren't words a guy would want to hear… but I feel wrong not saying them."

"Ok…" he says, waiting.

"I just want to be transparent, and let you know that yes I had lots of fun and yes I want to spend more time together and get to know you better….but … well… remember when I first met you I told you I was going on LOTS of dates?"

"Yes…"

"Well, I've stopped going on dates with new men, but, there are a few that I have been on multiple dates with. And for now, I'm still figuring it out. For all I know, you are too. Maybe you are going on other dates too, and it's not even my right to know yet. The other night… in the car when you dropped me off… I wanted to kiss you. But I didn't because I thought it would be wrong to do that if I wasn't sure. I'm sorry I'm telling you this."

Lucas jumps in, "No no no, don't be sorry. If ever in doubt, always be honest and forthcoming. And don't EVER let your girlfriends tell you to keep something from me."

I sense a bit of anger in his voice and it frightens me because it means he's irritated, frustrated, or… hurt.

"I'm sorry that I don't know for certain. I want to know for certain, but I don't."

"It's okay, I don't know for certain either."

"Ok, well... I have a way of getting myself into very awkward conversations. You might be a bit surprised, but I'm not."

He laughs, a little bit, quietly, and says, "So when can I see you again?"

"How about early this coming week?"

"I'm booked till Thursday or Friday," he replies.

"Ok, let's touch base mid-week then."

"Ok" he says.

As I drive away, I think about my initial reaction to having lots of men on the horizon at once. I think about the sheer glee. And then I think about how I feel right now.

I want to explore the Laughing Lucas on the horizon AND the Adventure Alex on the horizon. Maybe even the Older Oliver and the Med-School Mat too. But not all at once. Why did they have to come along all at once, forcing me to choose? How long can I put off the decision or will they end up making it for me?

As my cell phone rings, I realize my car radio has been playing on low and I've been ignoring it. The two sounds clash.

I ignore the call and turn off the car stereo. I blaze along the vacant highway in silence. I'm wanting for some quiet.

Saturday, February 13

WIPED OUT

I'm scheduled to tutor Lucille, but forget until about twenty-five minutes past our appointment time. I call and cancel. I've had a mild but persistent headache for the past two days and feel completely drained.

By afternoon, I'm too exhausted to be productive, so I log into Match. My Matchbox has twenty-two new messages. I feel like I'm being subjected to a steady slideshow of everything I can't have. It's hard to be content with what's in front of you when you're conveniently reminded every day via an unfailing string of emails of all that's still out there. I wonder if I'm missing out by putting a "hold" on meeting new men.

I've been messaging back and forth with an English bloke, but I've put off meeting. By the time I decide to click on his message, just to consider it, his profile is inactive. I feel relieved that this is an alley that I won't feel obligated to tread.

Sunday, February 14

THE POSTER CHILD
FOR VALENTINE'S DAY

Sunday mornings are my favorite occasions to jog. The Valley hosts a vast and marvelous (for a furniture fiend like myself) number of weekend yard sales. One Sunday I found a desk desperately in need of repair, attention, and a fresh coat of paint. I could see through the decay to a solid set of sturdy and stylistically striking bones. This desk had personality. I bought it and spent a week sanding and painting it in the backyard. Now it lives in my bedroom and I sit at it everyday.

The adoption of my desk brought me much joy, but there have been other "morning sightings" that have ended in heart-break. I don't have the storage space to amass an entire apartment's worth of furniture before actually moving. Therefore, I can't bring home every desk, chair, or table I fall in love with. I have to be very critical of each one I find, I have to really ask myself if I can't live without it. Because the choices are abundant, I'm aware I can't have them all.

I'm obviously not thinking about furniture here anymore.

I parade about the market-like neighborhoods, wearing hot pink sweats and a big pink and white-stripped ribbon in my hair. With so many suitors, I feel like the poster-child for Valentine's Day this year, so I figure might as well dress like it.

My mom calls in the afternoon. She's on vacation in Miami and wants to know the latest scoop. She is surprised when I don't mention Older Oliver.

I explain, "I haven't heard from him in awhile now, and during our last conversation, I invited him to Tess's birthday. He declined. The ball is in his court and he's letting it roll. Perhaps it's finally happening. The guys are starting to do the choosing."

At 7 pm sharp, Adventure Alex rings the doorbell, and I peer through the peephole before letting him in. He's standing confidently and casually, yet his boyish grin gives away his anticipation towards seeing me again. He's wearing a dark charcoal blazer, necessitated by our dinner date's formal venue. I step outside and follow him as he walks to the passenger side of his car and opens the door for me. He navigates the sharply curved roads of Topanga canyon like a professional racecar driver (and with what seems like almost the same speed). We arrive at The Inn of the Seventh Ray, and it is even more fairytale-esque than I had imagined. The outdoor seating patios step up and down along varying levels so that some tables seem to be isolated on their own raised islands. Monstrously large trees enclose the grounds into smaller alcoves with their leaning branches, creating privacy and intimate dining. The trees drip with white lights, and chandeliers hang from the open-sided white tents. The entire scene is enchanting.

I linger during dinner, slowly savoring the candied walnut and cranberry mixed greens salad, shrimp cervice, salmon, chardonnay, and Alex's company. We share stories from our travels, tidbits from our day, discuss again the stigmas surrounding online dating, and somehow, find ourselves talking about relationships past.

I ask him, frankly, "Have you ever been in love?"

Without hesitation, he replies, "Yes. I was fifteen when I met her..."

I can tell by the way his eyes light up and the care with which he says the word "her" that he must have loved her very much.

"Have you been in love?" he asks.

"Yes I've been in love. I was eighteen. We met in college and immediately sensed a connection. We wanted the same things from life, had similar goals, endless energy, big dreams, and so much in common."

Alex responds, "That's how it was in our case, too. We were both so motivated, and had so much in common."

"That doesn't mean it always works out though, does it?" I say.

"Apparently not," he replies.

I decide to be completely honest with him and explain, "I probably shouldn't tell you this, but I want to. On our last date, I intentionally threw you curveballs to see if you'd catch them, or dodge and run. I made a point to discuss my fear of ocean water that night at McDonalds specifically BECAUSE you said you loved to surf. I did it because even before I met you, when all I knew of you was your letters, I sensed the possibility that I could really fall for you. While "meeting you" through your written words, I felt a similar thrill to that which I felt when I first spoke to the ex-boyfriend who I loved but eventually lost. The feeling both delighted and terrified me. I think that's why I tried to sabotage the evening. On some level I'm resisting letting myself fall for fear of getting hurt again. I guess I was trying to shake things up to see if they'd easily shatter. I'm sorry," I say.

He looks at me for a few moments, perhaps searching my face for further clues, and then replies, "I had a feeling that's what you were up to. It's okay. I've been there. I've been in love and I've seen it end. You don't need to apologize."

After our entrée plates are removed, he leans in towards me and says, "Every time I read an email from you I can almost see the thoughts bouncing around in your head. I'm sure this is partly due to the color and size variations you implement. I'm guessing you do this because you are a designer. I don't remember the last time I met someone so full of life, energy, and imagination. It's so refreshing. Can I tell you a secret?"

I nod my head and Alex continues, "There are aspects of my personality I have repressed either intentionally or subconsciously and I feel like you know what they are and try to wrestle them out of me every time we talk. I knew the first time I met you that you and I were very different. I'm not looking for someone just like me. I used to think I was, and that girl I loved in high school was a lot like myself. That's not what I'm looking for now."

I reply, "I'm not looking for that anymore either."

"Can I tell you something else?" he asks.

"Of course" I reply.

He continues, "I have to admit I loved what you wrote in one of your letters about your siblings. I love that you're confident in them and proud of them. My younger sister just started at UC Irvine, so we currently live closer to each other than we have in years. I helped her apply to school, helped her pick out the one she wanted to go to, took her to her orientation, and dropped her off on her first day. I've been to almost all her ultimate Frisbee tournaments and we've even met up a few times just to hang out and go surfing. I'm finally starting to figure out who my little sister is and play a part in who she becomes. It's amazing."

We sit at the table talking long after the waitress takes the check and the candles have burned down to waning hints of flame. Alex drives me home, and walks me to the door. I don't kiss him goodnight. I want to, but I don't.

As soon as I close the door behind me, aunt Ellen, in her nightgown and slippers asks, "WELL? How was it?"

"Wonderful," I reply.

"Well, did you KISS him?" She asks.

"No, but I wanted to."

"GO CHASE DOWN HIS CAR AND GIVE HIM A GOODNIGHT KISS!!!! IF YOU DON'T I WILL!!!!"

I reply, "No, it's too late now. Besides, I don't know if it's right considering I'm still seeing Lucas and Mat."

"Oh my, Rachel! You are approaching this all wrong! In my generation there was NOTHING wrong with having lots of suitors! You don't put all your eggs in one basket! You don't even know if it has holes! What if you DID kiss him and it repulsed you? How are you to find out if you don't let yourself try? Why do you think it's wrong?"

"Because, I don't think they're going on dates with other women," I reply.

"Don't kid yourself," she replies, and walks away.

CLEAR SKIES AND HIGHS

TODAY I AM A DESIGNER.

For our green showcase home project, my partners and I collaborated with a textile company to design two new printed fabrics. At 1 pm today, the doorbell rings, and the fabric swatches arrive.

I know the contents of the package before opening it. I take it upstairs to my bedroom, suppressing the urge to bolt up five steps at a time. In the privacy of my room, I put the envelope on my bed, and pause. I want to remember this moment. It is a second graduation of sorts, propelling me into the company of other textile designers whose products currently grace the market. I open the wrapping and lay the fabrics out on my chaise. I inspect them carefully. Holding the pieces in my hands ignites a remarkable exhilaration. I predict that someday walking through a space or building of my own design is the only related experience that could possibly trump this one. Something I drew, something I imagined, is now real, and right in front of me. I drape it over the edge of my bed. I tack the largest swatch to my window to see how the light filters through the fibers. I pull another piece tightly around a pillow, I examine BOTH sides of the fabric, I view the two patterns next to each other, and I study the two patterns apart from each other. I do absolutely everything short of stripping off my clothes and wrapping myself in the swatches.

Before even calling the printer and CEO of the textile company to approve the swatches, I email images to my mother and two design partners to share the good news. In the corner of my screen, the weather widget shows "clear skies and highs in the upper 70s." Even the climate is celebratory! I had hoped to have a very productive day, but now want to do just that, celebrate. And, I'd like to have someone to celebrate with.

It's a national holiday so chances are Alex isn't working. I call to see if he'd want to join me for a gym-date and then picnic lunch in the park since it is SUCH a beautiful day.

He comes right over and I greet him in my front yard, fabric swatches in hand, too jazzed to wait inside.

I hold the pieces out in front of me so he can inspect them and explain rapidly, "I designed these. They JUST arrived. I'm stoked!"

"They're awesome!" he exclaims, with an enthusiasm that matches mine. It seems my energy has an infectious effect on him.

We drive to 24-hour fitness. He parks and moves to get out of the car but I grab his arm and say, "Wait."

"Yes?" he asks.

"I want to do something I meant to do last night but didn't."

I lean forward and kiss him.

He smiles and asks, "So why didn't you do that last night? You know I wanted to kiss you too."

"I was just putting too much thought into it. I even discussed it with aunt Ellen and she told me to go running out the door after you!"

"She did?!"

"Yep!" I say, smiling brightly.

"I like aunt Ellen. She told you to kiss me," he replies, grinning.

He leans in, and this time he kisses me.

We sit smiling at each other, until I shatter the moment by saying, "Ok, green light go!" and bolting from the car. He races me through the parking lot and into the gym.

"I'm going to elipticize. Reconvene in the yoga studio to stretch together post-cardio?" I ask.

"Sounds great. I'm going to run. See you in a bit!" he replies.

Later, dripping with sweat, we meet up in the yoga studio.

"How was your workout?" he asks.

"Excellent, lots of excited energy to burn."

"Right, of course," he replies, and then leans towards the floor, puts his weight on his arms, and extends his body into a handstand. This movement animates the many compartments of his well-defined back. He's shirtless, and the perspiration drips in non-linear paths as it navigates the topography of his deltoids, shoulder blades, and then trickles down across his abs and obliques.

He travels about the studio upside down, and then in a series of movements that look like a cross between karate and break dancing.

"What are you doing?" I ask, confused.

"Capoeira," he says with a smile, and explains that it's an Afro-Brazilian art form that is a cross between martial arts and dance. You-tube it. It's incredible to watch. He promises to take me to the studio where he studied Capoiera while in college.

After the gym we go to the park for a picnic lunch. I discover that Alex has a dislike for carrots which borders full blown "carrot phobia." Or, he's just exaggerating to make me feel less wimpy about fearing the ocean (among 1,203,385 other things).

The table is mostly in direct sunlight, and it is unrelenting on my cheeks, arms, and shoulders. I don't dodge the rays because I want to feel it in full saturation. On some level, I'm aware that I don't want to experience the "winds" from behind a glass window. What I mean is that I want to feel, not just observe life and love. The tree adjacent to our table reaches skyward in thankful salute and the leaves simmer from a faint, yet finicky breeze. I'm hoping for my cheeks to inch as close to that fine line between burn and pink as possible, without sentencing myself to pain in the morning. Weak sun is nice, but the best sun is the kind that you feel on your cheeks JUST before you burn. The sun drips light on my lashes and as I grasp for a word to describe this moment, I find "pleasure."

Children surround us, playing tag on the grass. Shouts of "Mine!" and "Got it!" echo from the pickup soccer game at the far end of the park. Closer to our picnic table, a father teaches his daughter to ride a two-wheeler. She has knee and elbow pads over her bunching pink sweat suit. Her helmet glitters with stickers. She sits rigid and looks petrified as her father pushes her along, hunched down grasping the seat to balance the teetering bike. Alex watches and remarks, "Ha! What are the chances of witnessing THAT? That is a VERY momentous occasion. Learning to ride a bike multiplies a kid's 'turf' by ten."

A pre-teen zig-zags by on a scooter, showing off for his friends, and face plants on the cement path. He looks embarrassed. One of his buddies zips past him, grooving to the tunes ringing from his I-pod ear buds.

I joke, "The kids I see here are SO MUCH COOLER than I was at their ages. Or than I EVER was as a kid. I'm not sure if it's something about California youth versus Virginia kids... or if I was just a really big loser. Although, if I was such a big loser back then, I was oblivious to my total loser status."

I recall the first time I was made aware of my "loser" status. It was also my first experience with dating, or, rather, my first attempt at it. In seventh grade I fell hard for one of the boys on my block. Every morning we'd walk to the bus stop together. Some mornings, I'd have my CD headphones on, playing Britney Spears' first album "Baby One More Time." Other times, we'd talk. On the last day of eighth grade, I finally mustered the courage to ask him if he wanted to by my boyfriend.

His response was: "No thank you."

On that summer afternoon when I sat in the awkward limbo between junior high and high school, if someone promised me that that instance wasn't foreshadowing my future dating life, I wouldn't have believed them. Further, if they had told me that one day I'd be sitting in a park, enjoying a picnic with someone as dashing as the man in front of me now, I wouldn't believe them either.

Alex and I don't fill every second with sound and we both seem to be comfortable with the occasional pauses in conversation. After we finish our sandwiches he says, "Stay right here, I'll be right back!" and rushes off towards his car. The sight evokes the memory of the first time I saw him. I recall him running through the rain in his coat and tie, along the banded windows of the coffee shop. His business clothes seemed to suit him just as well as well as the grungy gym clothes he wore when he picked me up this morning and the khakis and polo he's wearing now. I can picture him at ease in an executive boardroom, on an exotic safari excursion, on my arm in a tuxedo at a black tie affair, exploring the water caves of Belize, and lounging in boxers while reading beside me in bed of rumpled sheets on a lazy Sunday morning.

I'm not sure if I can picture him in my orange grove, it's too soon to tell.

He returns with an assortment of rock climbing ropes and proceeds to tie them around two trees. A small, curious audience of "cool kids" gathers nearby. He makes a tightrope, suspended about three feet in the air, jumps up, and begins to walk back and forth along it.

"Want to try?" he asks.

"Yes!" I exclaim as I kick off my shoes and reach for him to hoist me up. While I shakily inch along the rope he holds my hand so I can keep my balance.

When I'm ready to come down I ask him if he can help me. He picks me up off the rope, throws me over his shoulder, and begins to spin in circles.

As I watch my world blur to chaos below me, for the first time on a date, the analytical/questioning/critiquing part of my brain completely shuts off. Perhaps it's because I'm getting too dizzy from the spinning, or perhaps it's because I'm too entranced by the wild, control-less sensation of being swung around at invigorating speed.

We're having fun.

But I remember I have work to do. Something in my face must have just blown my cover, and conveyed the sneaking of my thoughts out of this lovely park and back to my projects.

"It's time for you to get back to work, yes?" he asks, proving how closely he is paying attention.

"Yes" I reply, and he drives me back home. I get out of the car and step up onto the curb. He comes around and stands on in the street, looking up at me. He kisses me.

As he retreats to his car, I call out, "That was a fun one, I was taller than you!" He laughs.

Once inside, I find uncle Carl and aunt Ellen entertaining guests in the kitchen.

"Hiya Kid, how's the date-scapades going?" Uncle Carl asks, sending a wink my way.

"Good, just got back from the park with Alex," I reply.

"Oh, the actor?" he asks.

"No" I reply.

He offers a second attempt, "The Med-Student?"

"No" I reply.

"The writer?"

"Nope, THIRD STRIKE uncle Carl! This date was with a cartographer," I reply.

He turns to his guests, our interested spectators, and explains, "She goes out with a different lad each night!"

Not quite… but almost. Turning away from aunt Ellen, I reach for a piece of chocolate covered toffee from the Ghirardelli box leftover from Valentine's Day. One of the guests remarks, "Ah, and she has quite the sweet tooth!"

Aunt Ellen replies, "No, she doesn't really snack on candy."

I open my palm and turn back towards aunt Ellen, showing the chocolates.

She looks surprised. I explain, "I've been craving something sweet lately."

She motions me in close, and whispers, "I bet you have!"

Tuesday, February 16

BEWARE OF THE KISS OF DEATH

I wake up with a pounding headache and sore throat. I call Alex and say "Good morning! Urgent, breaking news: today my throat was sore when I woke up and I have a mild headache. I'm hoping its allergies…the warm weather bringing seasonal change…but I'm not ruling out the beginning of a cold. I hope I wasn't the 'kiss of death' for you! Please eat a few oranges; they are FILLED with vitamin C! Maybe this is irrelevant because I'm having allergies? Can't be sure, but it's best to be prepared! If the situation changes and if I improve dramatically or plummet to the depths of bed-ridden ILLNESS, I'll let you know."

He laughs (consequently making me wonder if he thinks I'm insane) and replies, "Thanks for the heads up. I'll lick my zinc stone twice today and be especially wary of any symptoms. I have been taking a regular regimen of antibiotics and malaria pills from the Kenya trip, so maybe I'll escape this one. Though, even if I knew I would get sick from kissing you, I wouldn't have done anything differently."

"Okay" I say, deliberately accenting the single word with an audible smile. "Tonight is 'Taco Tuesday' and Tess has been bugging me for weeks to attend. I've declined the offer because I've been busy with work. If I'm feeling better by 7:30 would you want to join us?"

I'm horrid at math, but I'm apt enough to know that adding one boyfriend, but subtracting a few best friends does not equal a positive equation. It's important to me that my boyfriend get along with my girlfriends, and tonight could be the perfect opportunity to see if it all adds up as I hope it will. I realize this test could be more pressure inducing for Alex than requiring him to juggle fire batons or walk a tight-rope (the latter of which he already voluntarily passed, yesterday).

He replies, "That would be great, and I LOVE Tacos. I hope you feel better and that I get to see you tonight."

I decide right then and there that he will see me tonight, even if I come down with a full-fledged FLU. I'll just be sure not to kiss him, and maybe I'll wear a sanitary mask over my nose and mouth and sit a few booths away from him and my friends...

My mother calls and instructs me to "Cut down on the running and bulk up the sleeping." I know she's right, but I want to run to "jumpstart" my day so that I can be alert enough to be productive. I blatantly ignore her (more serious than a doctor's) orders, but my ailments slow me down and delay my run until almost 2 pm.

Instinctively, I race towards my orange grove. Once through the gate, I weave in and out of the rows. As I make a hard turn at the end of the last row, I'm startled to find the groundskeeper resting on one of the stone benches. Only a few feet separate us, we are closer than we have ever been. He is sitting very still; perhaps his arms are heavy from the morning's work. Usually, I see him in motion and at a distance of at least four rows, but it's much later than the time our paths usually cross, and if he was up at his (our) usual hour, he's been working for over six hours by now. Or maybe he was feeling ill this morning too, and had a late start as well.

I stop, and wipe the sweat from my forehead. "Good morning," I say cautiously.

"Good afternoon" he corrects me, kindly.

"Yes, good afternoon," I reply.

We exchange subtle smiles (the kind you make with your eyes and brows, not your mouth) and then I recommence my run with the awareness of his eyes following me out of the grove.

By afternoon my symptoms worsen. The mild morning headache slowly gains momentum until it reaches a heavy throb. Against the advice of aunt Ellen, I'm determined to keep my dinner plans. I'm the first to arrive at the restaurant so I wait out front for Alex.

He texts me: *"34.151310, -118.452021."*

"WHAT?" I reply.

He writes back: *"That's my present location. Geographic coordinates."*

(Figures, since he's a cartographer!)

A few minutes later he arrives and we don't kiss (my body language makes it apparent that I intend to keep my distance, for his protection, of course).

Once Tess and my other friends join us we all head inside to be seated. The restaurant is crowded, and loud. My head pounds. I introduce everyone to Alex. Tess is nice, and throws him a bone by asking him questions about the proposed extension of the LA metro line (which she knows he'd enjoy answering since the company he works for is involved in mass transit and urban planning consulting). She is attempting to put him at ease, and I'm appreciative.

Each time one of Tess' friends that I've never met arrives she introduces them to Alex and me. Each time I decline their handshakes, explaining I might be contagious.

To one of her friends I respond, "No really, if I wasn't sick I'd touch you," then, realizing how weird that sounds, I add, "Never mind."

I don't order any food because my throat is really sore at this point. When Alex finishes his tacos he looks over at me and asks, "Really not hungry?"

I whisper, "Throat too sore... I could go for soft serve... in fact I'll probably get it on my way home."

"Want to go now?" he asks.

"Yes! Would you like it for dessert?" I ask.

"Always," he replies.

He leaves his portion of the bill on the table and we make a beeline to the nearest McDonalds. As we walk in, he says, "I like this tradition we have now."

At our table, he laughs, "You were pretty funny every time someone tried to shake your hand."

"I don't want to get anyone sick. I'll feel horrible if I already got you sick!"

My legs are crossed and my foot is therefore at a diagonal, and hangs just to his lower right. While eating his ice cream, he reaches down and rubs my foot affectionately.

I joke, "I suppose my foot's not contagious."

A classic-rock song comes on the speakers and he sings along.

"Do you like to see tribute bands perform?" I ask.

"Oh yea!" he replies.

I'd like to see one with him.

When I get to the bottom of my ice cream cup he asks, "Time to get you home?"

"Yes," I croak.

We walk out and before parting he gives me a hug because I won't kiss him.

I fit perfectly in his arms.

Wednesday, February 17- Sunday, February 21

HIBERNATION

I spend the greater part of the next five days sleeping.

Aunt Ellen checks on me from time to time, and repeatedly tells me "You've been burning your candle at TOO many ends."

She's right.

On Friday, in the black of my darkened bedroom, I watch my phone light up on the bedside table. I reach for it; it reads "Match Alex." I screen it.

An hour later, I text him;

"Confession: I screened your call. Throat too sore."

On Saturday night, I finally call him.

"Sorry for screening," I say.

He replies, "Don't worry about it, I understand you haven't felt up to talking. Besides, I've been away- skiing! The rain we had last night laid down a fresh coat of power on the mountain. It was great, but I miss you Sunshine!"

I've been too sick to run. I miss my orchard.

I reply, "Listen, you're going to have to stop calling me that. It makes me smile every time you say it and I'm going to get horrible wrinkles from too much smiling."

"As far as calling you Sunshine is concerned, you're just going to have to deal with the wrinkles. I'm kind of an immediate satisfaction type guy, and getting a smile out of you now, at the cost of a few wrinkles down the road is completely worth it."

Each night I go to bed, there's a "Sweet dreams Sunshine" message from him, and a "Good morning Sunshine" one to greet me when I wake.

In the successive nights of Nyquil-induced, fantastical-dream-filled-heavy-as-a-log, comatose sleep, I have vivid dreams of my orchard… and of Alex.

Monday, February 22

DAY BREAK

Today my head feels like the streets look after a week of constant rain. There's still a bit of fog (the transition from downpour to clear skies is sluggish), but I'm feeling much more clear-minded. True, my gutters are still a bit clogged, but the pounding has given way to a bit of calm.

I spend the day catching up on correspondence and freelance work. I don't dare attempt a run, but I sure as hell want to. I decide that tomorrow I will actually get dressed, leave my house, go to work, and… see Alex.

I call him after dinner and he answers, "I'm glad you called! I want to tell you about a meeting I had today at the old Santa Fe train depot in San Bernardino. It's a beautiful old building; I think you would really like it. Standing in the main terminal made me feel like I was a businessman from the twenties, traveling to LA from Chicago on an overnight Santa Fe passenger express train. It's like a scene right out of Atlas Shrugged. It even has a coffee shop where I can easily imagine Dagny Taggart sitting!"

(As soon as he speaks the words 'coffee shop', I'm already picturing her sitting there.)

I reply, "That sounds awesome. We should go explore the station together sometime. Make an adventure out of it! So, guess what I did today?"

"What?" he asks.

"Well, I guess it's not something I actually did, but something I realized. I realized I haven't roasted any marshmallows this winter! My first smore-less winter! Very strange for a Virginia girl!"

Alex jumps in, "There are fire pits at the beach just south of where I live! We could roast marshmallows there!"

"Can we go tomorrow after work?" I ask excitedly.

"Absolutely!" he replies.

Tuesday, February 23

BON FIRE

After work I drive to Alex's. We load the car with logs, hot dogs, graham crackers, chocolate, and marshmallows, and drive south to Playa del Rey. Apparently, that's the only beach in LA County where you can have an open fire. Adventure Alex, as a cartographic-MAPMAN, knows these sorts of things.

We find a vacant pit and Alex builds a fire. I feel like we are secluded in a cozy room that only extends as far as the warmth of the flames. Beyond the walls of this intimate hearth, manifestations of natural and man-made beauty reflect directly across from each other. On one side the ocean roars while on the other side of us cars rush by. The road leads up to clusters of cavernous houses lit like constellations on the steep hillside.

More lights twinkle on the inhabited cliff than in the sky. From time to time an airplane jets overhead as it approaches LAX. Preparing to land, the planes are so low that they appear like the undersides of whales gliding in a dark ocean above. I imagine I'm on the sea floor, looking up. Each time a plane passes overhead the propellers' volume causes trembles in my chest and drowns out our voices. I think of the passengers peering through the windows and wonder if our fire has caught their attention, and if they see us as two tiny dots in a surreal, miniature world below.

It's juxtaposition, the ocean and the parking lot, the crashing of waves and the engines of planes. Yet nothing seems out of place, and even the haloed parking lot lights look divine.

We sit on the concrete edge of the fire pit and roast our skewered hot dogs and marshmallows. The flames dance merrily from the tidal winds. The fire illuminates Alex's face, making the darkness behind him dissolve into an abyss.

After we finish eating, Alex pulls out a light-up Frisbee and attempts a game of catch with me. Unfortunately each time I throw it, he ends up chasing it for several yards down the beach, while each time he throws it (almost directly) to me, I end up missing it, falling into the sand, and laughing until I'm out of breath.

When our sides really start to hurt and we're gasping for air more than actually playing catch, we collapse on the quilt in the sand. I lie down and put my feet up on the ledge of the hearth, to steal heat from the fire. Alex is sitting, and I rest my head in his lap and stare up at the sky. Alex is looking down at my face, playing with my hair.

"You've worn those pearl earrings every time I've seen you. They suit you. You wear them well," he says.

"Thank you" I say, and then, searching his face and finding a steady smile, I ask, "Do you think you were born happy?"

"I don't really think people are born with emotions. I was hungry or sleepy or curious, not happy or sad."

"Oh Alex, that's not what I meant at all. I didn't mean it scientifically. Wow we think about things so differently. What I meant was…you're a very happy person. I was asking if you were always that way, or if you learned to be that way later in life. I'm always curious about how different people come to know happiness, whether it's inherent and innate or if it's something they had to find."

He answers "Oh, okay. To answer the question in the way I think you meant it, well, my parents were happy and I was surrounded by happy people. I always remember being optimistic."

While resting with my head in his lap and listening to him talk, I wonder how long the sand will remember the weight of our bodies.

He leans down and kisses me, hard. I warned him I might still be a little bit sick but that doesn't seem to deter him. I kiss him back because I want to, and because I know he wants me to. My hands are cold, and he holds them in his to keep them warm. My fingers find their way to the small of his back, a little cove of heat.

"Are your hands always this cold?" he asks.

I reply, "Usually. Are yours always so warm?"

"Usually."

He lies down next to me, so we're side by side gazing up at the star-less, polluted, lovely Los Angeles sky.

I whisper, "I want to make this another habit of ours."

I relish in my self-sufficiency, but can see myself growing emotionally connected to him. Is it possible to be both rapt and independent?

Above us, another plane rumbles by as if challenging the crashing waves below.

In Alex's arms I feel protected from the wind, but know I can break away at any minute to feel it again in full force against my chilled cheeks.

I remain still. For this moment, I let him captivate me.

CALL OFF THE TROOPS

I'm falling for Alex and know I need to tell Laughing Lucas and Med-School Mat. I decide to relay the message via email, so that they'll have time to let my words sink in before responding. As I hit the keys, my fingers drag and resist the motions. I know it's the right thing to do, but it feels wrong and unkind.

I write:

As you know, I met lots of men through my MATCH.COM adventure. I WANTED to meet LOTS of people because I wanted to know what was out there. The tricky part was that (huge shocker) I didn't just meet one person that I got along well with.

I was hoping I'd meet lots of people, find ONE, and upon first meeting them-just KNOW... and end the search, so to speak.

Perhaps that was a juvenile fantasy.

The point I'm trying (or trying not) to get to is that I have met someone on Match and I'd like to really see where it could go.

Perhaps that's more information than you wanted, I'm not sure. Perhaps you just want to be friends with me, and this email is unnecessary and therefore pleasantly awkward. (I hope so.)

I have had a lot of fun getting to know you and I would like to have you as a friend.

Maybe that's too much to ask.

Feeling like a Debbie downer,

Rachel

Lucas responds:

Ms. Downer,

No worries, lady. I'm sincerely happy for you and I would love to be your friend. Thank you again for your honesty. You're rad.

Lucas

Mat responds:

Hey Rachel,

That's great! I am really happy for you! First, do not feel bad at all. Second, I would love to be a friend of yours if you would like.

-Mat

Wow, no frogs here, only princes.

RETURN TO THE ORCHARD

In an effort to return to good health ASAP, I have abstained from running for the past two weeks. Today, I feel ready.

At the orchard, the groundskeeper is busy with his morning chores. As per our typical custom, I race past without a word so as not to disturb him. I can tell he's content that I've returned to my normal routine.

The orchard is exactly as I remember it, except for the first time I notice a wooden sign that reads, "The beauty of this park is entrusted to you."

I think of Alex. I think of bringing him here, "entrusting" this beauty to him. It's to soon to consider, too soon to share with him this deeply personal place. It's too soon for him to know the foundation of my persona, the personal groves of my mind, the events, experiences, and beliefs that have crafted and contributed to the person I am today. Perhaps step one is sharing with him who I am now; the fruit of my journeys so far. As for revealing the sources, and letting him understand how I came to be the way I am, well, that can come later in its on time.

I stop running and reach down to collect an orange to bring to Alex. Each one seems a bit premature, not yet developed to its full potential of sugary sweetness. I spend a good ten minutes sorting through the fallen crop. I respect these trees too much to actively pick from their branches. I prefer to choose from the ones the trees have shed to share.

I race home carrying the ripest orange and stow it in my car so I won't forget to deliver it.

In the afternoon, I drive to Alex's apartment so that we can trek down to Irvine for a hot air balloon ride. I'm so excited to see him that I miss the turn onto his street. Twice.

I pull up, and he jumps into my car. Usually he drives, but this balloon ride was my idea so I insist on driving. I turn the radio up, explaining, "I made a CD of songs I think you might like."

New relationships are a lot of guess and check.

My guesses are right-on. We spend the entire trip rocking out.

At the park, it's too windy for balloon rides. I apologize for the weather, for the "ruined" plan, but he's not upset in the slightest.

"Listen, I was most excited about spending time with YOU, and that's what I'm doing, RIGHT NOW, so don't worry about the balloon ride, we're still having fun."

He's right. In fact, since we don't have to wait in the balloon line, we're free to explore the balloon park and then sit and rest on the cement path leading towards the balloons. A line of directional lights shoot away from us, towards the balloon lit in the distance, and it reminds me of an airplane runway.

I think of the night exactly one week ago, when we had our bonfire at the beach near the airport. I take pleasure in my sudden awareness that we're building a bank of shared memories capable of inducing familiarly comforting moments of déjà vu. He brushes my hair out of my face and puts it behind my ear. I love when he does that.

When I get too cold to remain outside, we walk back to my car. Alex puts his arm around my shoulders, and I lean away for a second just to see if he draws me back close. He does.

I let him drive, and somehow the icicle fingers of my left hand find their way into the hearth of his right palm. I don't realize my hand is curled in his until my fingers are nearly thawed.

"This makes me wish my car was automatic," he says.

"What?" I ask.

"My car is a stick-shift, so I wouldn't be as able to hold your hand while driving."

"Oh," I say, smiling in the darkness and turning to watch the mile-markers blur past through the closed passenger-side window. I leave my hand in his.

When we arrive at Alex's, I follow him into his house to get a drink of water before embarking on my long drive back to the Valley. In the frame of his doorway, I lean in to kiss him goodbye. Abruptly, I remember the orange I put in my car earlier this morning.

Just before our lips touch, I step back, and begin hurry away from him.

He tries not to look startled but his face betrays his confusion.

I call back over my shoulder "Wait a moment; I'll be right back!"

I run to my car and fetch the orange. I return to Alex's doorway and explain, "Here, this is an orange from a groove near my house. It might not be ready yet, it might need some time, but here..."

I reach my arm up to hold the fruit between us, and slowly move it closer to his face so he can he can inhale the vibrant perfume of citrus.

I smile, and laugh, "But doesn't it already smell delightful?"

IN CONCLUSION:

This book really doesn't have an ending, because it's not a story.

What about the men who's narratives I borrowed to fill these pages? The "not-characters"?

I hope that if they find their way to this book, it leaves them aware of the level of attention I paid to every second I spent getting to know them. I wish for my written words to convey the warm regard with which I recall the encounters and the lessons I learned from both the moments and the men.

And, as for me?

I can't predict what will come next, and I won't make it up.

Perhaps, like my first love, my relationship with Alex will end in pain.

However, I'm okay with that because for now, no matter how horrid the traffic during my morning commute is, how uncertain I am about the years ahead, or how exhausted I may find myself from not only everything I'm currently juggling but also from the thought of all I have yet to accomplish- on a daily basis I'm sincerely…

delighted.

"I tell you this to break your heart,

by which I mean only that it break open

and never close again."

Mary Oliver

Made in the USA
Charleston, SC
07 December 2010